Piering around Britain

A 'not-for-anoraks' photographic tour of all the surviving UK pleasure piers

John Choopani

Clacton-on-Sea

Bangor

Ramsey

Blackpool
Central

Great Yarmouth
Britannia

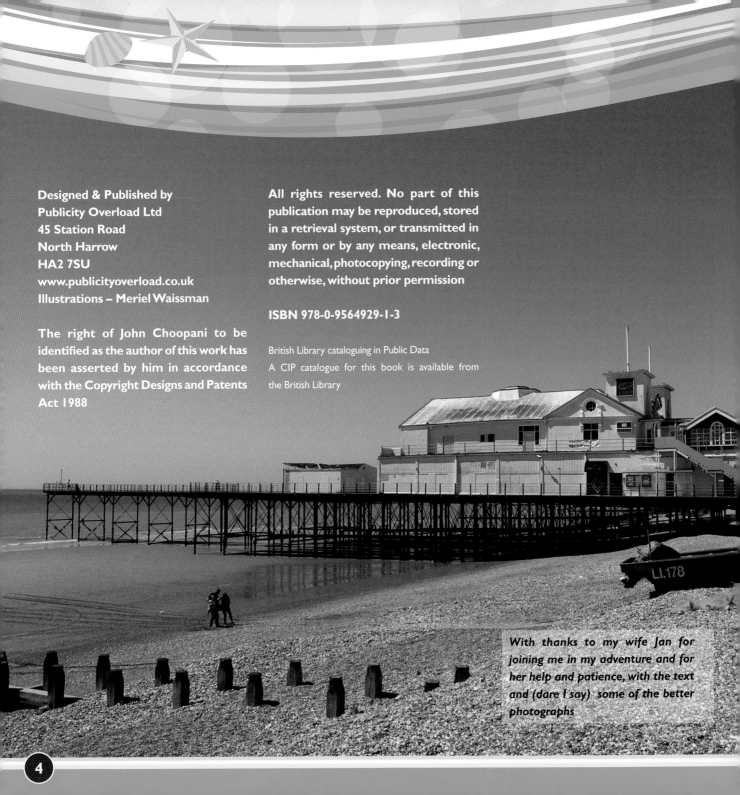

Designed & Published by
Publicity Overload Ltd
45 Station Road
North Harrow
HA2 7SU
www.publicityoverload.co.uk
Illustrations – Meriel Waissman

ISBN 978-0-9564929-1-3

British Library cataloguing in Public Data
A CIP catalogue for this book is available from the British Library

With thanks to my wife Jan for joining me in my adventure and for her help and patience, with the text and (dare I say) some of the better photographs

Contents

Piering around Britain

Introduction

Traditionally, a visit to a pleasure pier has played an important part in the enjoyment of seaside holidays, for both the young and the not-so-young.

There's always something of interest on a pier, whether it's simply a stroll over the waves with an ice cream, an opportunity to catch a free meal, the chance of winning at the amusements, or the challenge of a white-knuckle ride.

In their Victorian heyday there were around 100 pleasure piers distributed around the UK coast.

Thanks to wealthy Victorians and their growing desire for ozone, many investors in railways and ferry boats were also keen to invest in piers. This gave them the chance to sell more tickets by travelling to resorts which were previously inaccessible by sea. When purchasing the land required for the pier itself, these companies sometimes also built pier-front hotels by which to further benefit from their travellers. In some cases, they even provided hoists to ease access (for example at Saltburn, which was later replaced by an incline tramway). All of these things also brought wealth to the seaside town.

By giving visitors the opportunity to literally walk over the sea, these new piers were soon proving to be tourist attractions in themselves, especially in resorts with large tidal ranges, where for long periods of the day the sea couldn't even be seen.

As the popularity of piers boomed, so did the amenities offered on them: gas (then electric) lighting; entertainment; food and drink; theatres; bandstands dancing and pier parties. A pier was becoming an essential part of a seaside town and popular resorts such as Blackpool and Brighton boasted three!

Southwold Pier a rare success story

During my three year visit to all these surviving icons of the past, I have encountered many people who feel very passionate about the state of UK piers, yet still they continue to degenerate.

Although some are profitable commercial enterprises, many are not. Now less than 60 remain, and many of those are under threat. The increasing upkeep and maintenance costs will certainly ensure that many more are doomed.

I started my mission to see and photograph all the remaining piers primarily to visit many places in the UK that I hadn't been to before. But I am now one of the many enthusiasts who also feel passionately towards our UK piers.

I much regret that so many have fallen and hope that by sponsorship, government funding, lottery hand-outs and the tremendous efforts of pier enthusiasts locally and further afield, many more may reach their great potential to benefit their surrounding towns by drawing crowds to enjoy them.

LLANDUDNO

BRIGHTON

ROTHESAY

Why?

Why trek around the country looking at and photographing piers? Why indeed and why the fascination?

It didn't go back to fond childhood memories with bucket and spade on the beach playing under the barnacle-clad, decaying, rustic supports, nor the penny arcades; all the pennies have gone now John and NO, you can't have any more!!!

No, in fact, it started much more recently, on a winter break in Eastbourne in November 2009. We stayed at a sea-front hotel with sash windows that rattled in the windy and very wet conditions. There was a good view of the pier from our room and despite being continually pounded by the sea it looked very welcoming with its illuminations stretching out to sea.

Penarth Pier

Worthing Pier

Eastbourne

Eastbourne pier is an attractive structure. Although it was deserted when I visited in November., it wasn't difficult to visualise how a bit of sunshine would produce the hustle and bustle one associates with a popular seaside pier in a popular seaside resort, as the pictures taken during an earlier visit clearly show.

As you'd expect, a walk along the pier in November was very bracing. To a novice like myself, Eastbourne pier certainly seems to be very well preserved. It even has a camera obscura at the sea end, unfortunately closed in November, and I was overall very impressed with the pier.

However, the following day (again in gale force conditions), we visited Hastings, which was actually closed to the public so had a very different look. A campaign was in full flow to save the pier, which looked very sorry for itself and this was *before* the fire that engulfed it completely in 2010.

But the obvious passion to save the pier at Hastings did get me wondering how many piers there were and in what condition were all the others?

As with Estate Agent window browsing, most of these thoughts we have on holiday, are soon forgotten. But there was obviously a level of interest engendered in me and once home a Google search revealed all; a wealth of information about piers. And there was

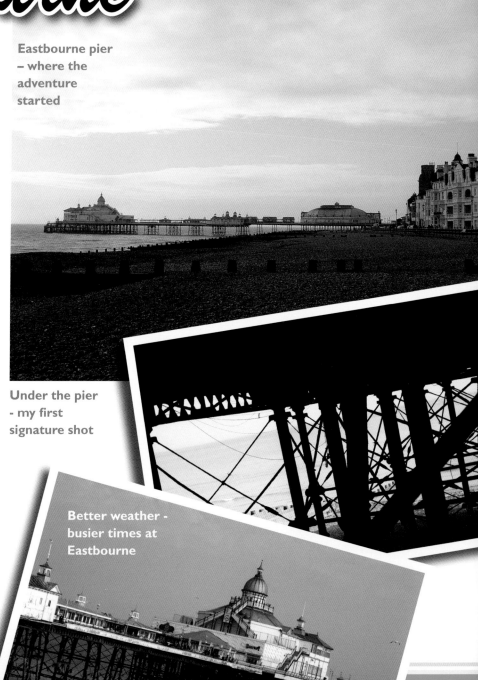

Eastbourne pier – where the adventure started

Under the pier - my first signature shot

Better weather - busier times at Eastbourne

Hastings

even a National Piers Society (NPS). So much information, surely a quest must begin?

Joining the society was an obvious place to start and for a £16.00 subscription I would receive a quarterly Pier Magazine and a membership card, (which I thought I'd better keep to myself, in case friends thought I was becoming an anorak). I was also surprised to learn how piers seem to evoke very personal feelings, whether they are tranquil retreats, commercial pleasure palaces, or simply an opportunity to fish for a free lunch. I was also impressed by how many people are keen to find out more and share their information

through the NPS. So much so, that I now welcome the Society's quarterly publication with relish.

To vindicate everything, at Christmas my wife, Jan, gave me a folder with a list of existing and defunct piers and some books she'd purchased from the National Piers Society. So my interest was now officially endorsed and my "Pier Mission" was about to commence.

In January 2010 my decision was made to visit and photograph all the NPS listed surviving piers. Not all in one whistle stop tour, but by a more leisurely mix of day trips, weekends away

and holidays around the UK's coastal resorts. This pace would also be more appealing to Jan, as I wanted some companionship along the way. I was quickly becoming aware that the UK pleasure pier was, in fact, quite unique. They were originally built not only to provide resort access for lucrative steam ship passengers, but also for the sheer enjoyment of promenading over the sea and seeing the waves, wildlife and land from a different perspective. Say what you like about kiss-me-quick hats, candy floss and good old British fish and chips, we are the best at all of them. I can't think of many people I know who can resist a stroll along a pier if there is one in (or near) a resort they are visiting.

This thought was reinforced, when I went on a tour to the West Coast of America and visited the pier at Santa Barbara. It seemed to be more of a car park rather than a place of enjoyment. And the American interpretation of seaside fish and chips leaves a lot to be desired. However the bird life was very different from our abundance of noisy, ever-scrounging seagulls.

As I'd now learnt that there were only 59 piers still existing, it wasn't long before I'd convinced myself that pier spotting as a long term project would ensure some interesting, and leisurely trips around the UK's coastline. Mind you, as you will see, some trips were less leisurely than others!

I'd already photographed Eastbourne and Hastings, albeit in gloomy November weather, but luckily I had taken shots of the Eastbourne pier during a visit in the summer of 2007, so definitely one to tick off.

Hastings didn't present itself with too many photo opportunities (being closed to the public). Sadly, since the fire

Santa Barbara – pier or car park?

Seagulls US style – bigger and better??

A fish and chip lunch, but not as we know it

Can Hastings really still be saved?

Danger Of Falling Debris

PIERS AUTUMN 2010
of the NATIONAL PIERS SOCIETY
STINGS PIER INFERNO
FULL COVERAGE INSIDE

ISSUE No: 106
PIERS
The Journal of the NATIONAL PIERS SOCIETY
WINTER 2012

Phase 1: Enhanced Old Pavilion

The remaining Old Pavilion is the only 'survivor' of the fire. The redevelop into a quality food and beverage establishment enterprise. Opening walls allows direct connections to the outs to seasons and weather.

Featuring: Hastings Hits The Jackpot!

Hastings after the fire

Photo courtesy Marlinova Collection

Bad and good news for Hastings

at Hastings in October 2010 there are now even less. So that's number two completed.

But, I understand there is some good news for Hastings. In May 2012 the first plans for the restored pier were published by the Hastings Pier and White Rock Trust who were, at the time, planning to purchase the remains of the pier for development. It's not long before I learn that there are many piers changing hands or under threat.

Well that's two piers completed then and with 59 piers still surviving according to the NPS ,that means there are 57 to go. So where to now?

Living north west of London and just three miles from Rickmansworth, (which I have been reliably informed is about the furthest point away from the coast you can actually live in the UK), there were no piers locally to head for.

We do, however, have a static caravan based near Woodbridge in Suffolk which we regularly visit. So for our first real pier experience since the mission was officially launched, we went for a day trip to Great Yarmouth which had two piers to offer, so both easily accessible in a day.

Great Yarmouth

For those who know Great Yarmouth, the resort offers a very wide sandy beach, so both the Britannia and Wellington Piers are usually just perched on dry land, not a vision I particularly associated with a seaside pier. The Wellington Pier was originally much longer (well, it had to be!) and the wooden skeleton stumps protruding from the end of the pier into the sea are still very visible.

The good news is that both piers seem to be thriving. The Britannia takes the form of a typical amusement centre with numerous attractions, popular bar and an over-the-sand theatre featuring a good assortment of well-known variety acts. In fact, a pier looking very much like a pier should and the donkey rides being taken on the sand below ensured my photos depicted a very traditional seaside scene.

The current pier was the second to be built on the site, the first was partly destroyed by a ship collision, hard to imagine as it appears to be mainly built on dry land. But in spite of the collision and more than its fair share of fires, it seems to be a popular venue now.

The Wellington Pier, which looks to have been recently refurbished, is primarily a bowling alley, also perched on the sand, but again in excellent

Britannia Pier, but where's the sea?

Britannia

Donkeys on parade

The pier entertainment – plenty of laughs all round

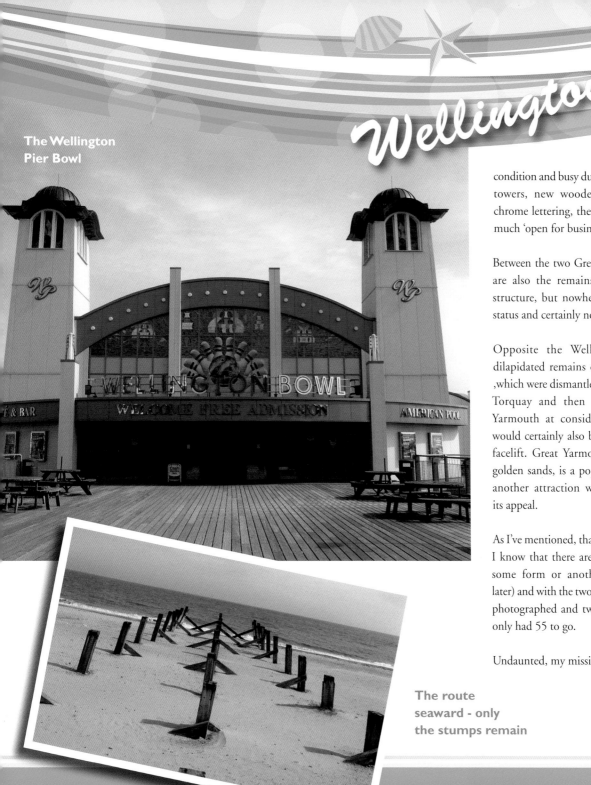

**The Wellington
Pier Bowl**

condition and busy during our visit. With twin towers, new wooden decking and smart chrome lettering, the Wellington is also very much 'open for business'.

Between the two Great Yarmouth piers there are also the remains of another pier-type structure, but nowhere near "pleasure pier" status and certainly not listed by the NPS.

Opposite the Wellington Pier are the dilapidated remains of the Winter Gardens ,which were dismantled and transported from Torquay and then reassembled at Great Yarmouth at considerable expense. These would certainly also benefit from a complete facelift. Great Yarmouth, with its miles of golden sands, is a popular family resort and another attraction would certainly add to its appeal.

As I've mentioned, thanks to the NPS web site I know that there are 59 piers remaining in some form or another, (more about that later) and with the two at Great Yarmouth duly photographed and two already ticked off I only had 55 to go.

Undaunted, my mission was underway.

**The route
seaward - only
the stumps remain**

Southwold

As a regular visitor to the Suffolk coast, my favourite reasonably local pier is the one at Southwold. But this time my trip there was going to be more than just a visit, it was now going to be part of my pier project. Following its complete renovation, the pier needed to be photographed and experienced.

Southwold is a charming, up-market, north Suffolk resort, certainly at one time (and maybe still) boasting the most expensive beach huts available in the UK. The town has very strong links with the sea, having a working lighthouse, busy harbour, attractive beach, hill-top cannon and, of course, that all-important pier. With a mixture of concrete and wooden supports and simple lines, the pier has been built to resemble a pier from the past, and this it certainly achieves.

Southwold Pier is very new; the current pier was only opened in 2001, though it has been built on the site of an earlier pier originally opened in 1900. The new pier can be singled out from other piers by its range of quirky amusements in its 'Under-the-Pier Show' which include a Bathyscape,

The water clock is one of a number of quirky Southwold exhibits

A rare pier success story

Colourful beach huts and the famous lighthouse

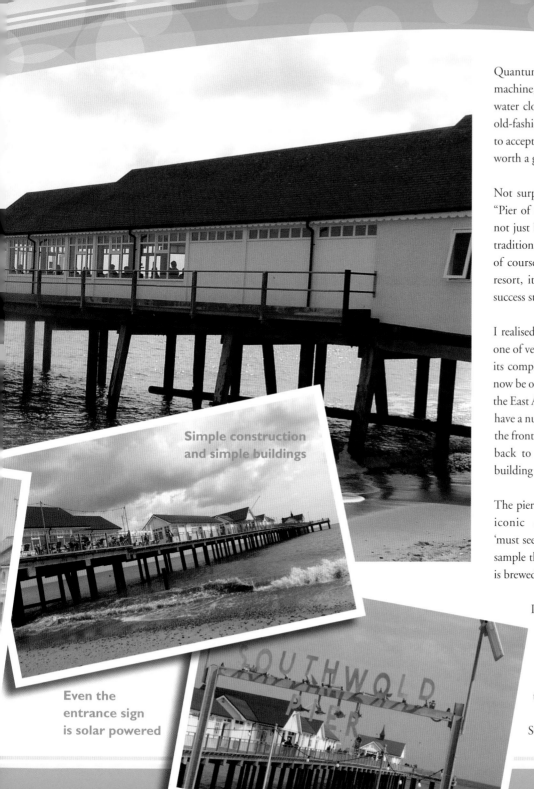

Quantum Tunnelling Telescope, Auto Frisk machine, automatic dog walker and amusing water clock. In fact there's a whole range of old-fashioned amusements - all now adapted to accept silver instead of copper - but all well worth a go.

Not surprisingly, Southwold won the NPS "Pier of the Year" competition in 2002 and not just because it was new. With its simple traditional looks and quirky attractions, plus of course the popularity of Southwold as a resort, it looks as though it's a pier with a success story to tell.

I realised later that Southwold appears to be one of very few true pier success stories. Since its complete refurbishment in 2008, it must now be one of the major tourist attractions on the East Anglian coast. There are even plans to have a number of holiday apartments built, at the front of the pier, but although I have been back to Southwold I have yet to see any building work commencing.

The pier also provides beautiful views of the iconic Southwold lighthouse another 'must see' on the Suffolk coast, and why not sample the excellent local Adnams ale which is brewed there?

I've also found out that the 2013 AGM of the National Piers Society is going to be held in Southwold in June so it's very likely to get another visit very soon. (Which I am pleased to say it did!)

So where to next?

Simple construction and simple buildings

Even the entrance sign is solar powered

Clacton-on-Sea

Keeping Woodbridge as my base, it seemed sensible to visit all the piers easily accessible from there. Clacton-on-Sea and Walton-on-the-Naze could comfortably be visited in a day trip. They are only 15 miles or so away as the seagull flies, but with all the river inlets of the Orwell, Stour and Deben, the travelling distance is nearly 50!

To Clacton-on-Sea first. A very different type of pier to the sophistication of Southwold, but in accord with my recollections of seaside piers in my youth. Yes, an amusement arcade on stilts with a fun fair to boot. It was a thriving place on a bright Sunday in May; noisy, boisterous and heaving with excited children having fun. Clacton pier is a higgledy piggledy construction on sturdy concrete pillars, but serving a very important purpose, judging by the level of activity I could see. I have to say, as far as I am concerned, it's definitely functional rather than attractive.

As with many pleasure piers the land end is a carpeted amusement arcade and a very busy one at that. In turn this leads out to an on-board funfair with roundabouts, dodgems and a delightful looking helter-skelter, with a corridor of stalls and side shows in between.

Once you've ventured past the amusement arcades and funfair there is a good old fashioned section of traditional wooden pier planking. You do get the feeling of walking over the sea, but sadly the planks aren't looking their best. So far, this fairly busy pedestrian walkway has luckily escaped attention from Health and Safety officialdom.

The traditional helter-skelter ride

Clacton-on-Sea pier overview

Clacton Pier under view

Walton-on-the Naze

Walton Pier stretching far out to sea

Beach huts stacked for that important sea view

Walton Pier - the frontage is the focal point of the town

A proper pier to promenade along

The stalls at Clacton also inspired my wife Jan to set up her own mission, to purchase a fridge magnet from every pier we now visit. This proved to be an ideal venture for her; combining a new hobby with fresh opportunities for some retail therapy along the way.

The next pier, and close by to Clacton, was Walton-on-the-Naze, which seems to form the focal point for the town. The bright, modern, colourful front section dominates the sea front. One of my favourites so far, Walton pier is divided into two very different halves. The front section is similar to that of Clacton, a very large and busy amusement arcade, full of joy; whilst the seaward half is very much a 'walking over the sea' experience.

The pier (which I now know is the third longest in the UK) has a definite curve and with its traditional wooden planking is certainly worth a visit. The views from the pier, coupled with a stroll along the promenade with the brightly coloured and imaginatively named beach huts, made for a very enjoyable day.

Next would be another pier relatively near to our caravan; Felixstowe.

Felixstowe

I remember visiting Felixstowe some time ago and then the residents were complaining about how the local council would be better off restoring their pier, rather than expensively block-paving and pedestrianising the high street. Looking at the sorry state of the pier now, it's obvious their voices were not heard, or certainly not listened to.

It seems people talk fondly about piers and find them real attractions, whether they are young or old, local residents or visitors. There's also something very traditional about the seaside pier and I am beginning to think every resort should now have one.

As the pictures show, the pier is long (2400 feet to be precise), and in its heyday had a railway running along its length. Nowadays, apart from the 50 feet or so of amusement arcade at the front, the main pier is closed to the public and is likely to remain so for some time, unless a great deal of money is invested in its repair and renovation.

I returned to Felixstowe in May 2013 to see the Ipswich to Felixstowe

Felixstowe pier dwarfed by the container port behind

Felixstowe - the new cafe, and railings separating it from the derelict rear section

The amusements - business as usual

Good solid reinforced concrete columns support the decaying decking above

The
Brig

Picture supplied by Richard Riding

The proposed new
Felixstowe Pier

vehicle run, an annual event when many interesting veteran, vintage cars and commercial vehicles make the journey and are then exhibited along the sea front.

More importantly, I am pleased to report that a small area of the disused exterior is now being used as an outside cafe so maybe there are plans afoot for Felixstowe.

In fact I have since found out that in October 2012 Suffolk County Council approved plans to build a new pier at Felixstowe with a futuristic design which could be open by 2014.

Let's hope.

So now that's eight piers completed in under six months and I've not have to travel far. Though looking at the list, this may well be changing soon if I really am going to visit and photograph every surviving pier.

Paignton

It looks like the dust-carts have just cleaned the beach

Ne...
day
dec
tak
to
the
alo
sur

It's
suc
cou
dec
refr
this

As
wer
sun

A p
dec
Suc
wor
to a
So
nov
seer

But
thei
of
sup
list

The next day we headed for Paignton. We were intending to take the boat to Paignton and then board the train to Dartmouth on the famous coastal railway. But the weather, (or more likely the lack of bottoms on seats) meant the boat wasn't sailing that day. As we'd strolled down to the front and left the car at the top of the hill we used the bus instead, which also gave me the opportunity to use my travel pass for the first time away from the London Underground. Some consolation for the passing of years!

Paignton – all in good shape

We walked down to the pier which was, I'm pleased to say, much more like I was anticipating; a proper pier pointing out to sea with amusements and rides....oh joy. It looked in good condition too, as did the resort.

The last time I came to Paignton was probably 35 years ago when the town was hosting a Waste Management conference, so the open spaces along the sea front were full of refuse carts, waste compactors and rubbish disposal systems, as well as an entourage of suited and booted sales personnel. Thankfully, it's much more pleasant without them.

I was also pleased to see that the pier looked in decidedly good condition and was attracting an encouraging number of visitors, though nobody was playing crazy golf in the open rear section

Photos duly taken, we moved on to Dartmouth and a delightful place it is, but sadly missing a pier.

Well decked out

PAIGNTON PIER

Anyone crazy enough for golf?

Teignmouth

A very typical
seaside pleasure pier

The following day we met one of my sons and family at Teignmouth. This is another proper seaside resort with a proper seaside pier, along similar lines to Paignton. Living in Bridgwater with two young children, trips to the seaside are frequently on their itinerary; Teignmouth has it all, without being too commercialised.

Like Paignton, the pier has a selection of amusements and rides and on a sunny Sunday was very busy. There was even a group of Morris-type dancers performing just outside.

There's no mistaking you are entering a pier when you get to the entrance, but like most other piers it has seen better times. In its heyday the pier had a pavilion at both ends providing entertainment in the form of tea dances, magic lantern shows and concerts. The pier was also the dividing line between male and female bathers at the resort: men's bathing machines to the west and

Fairground fun for
the children

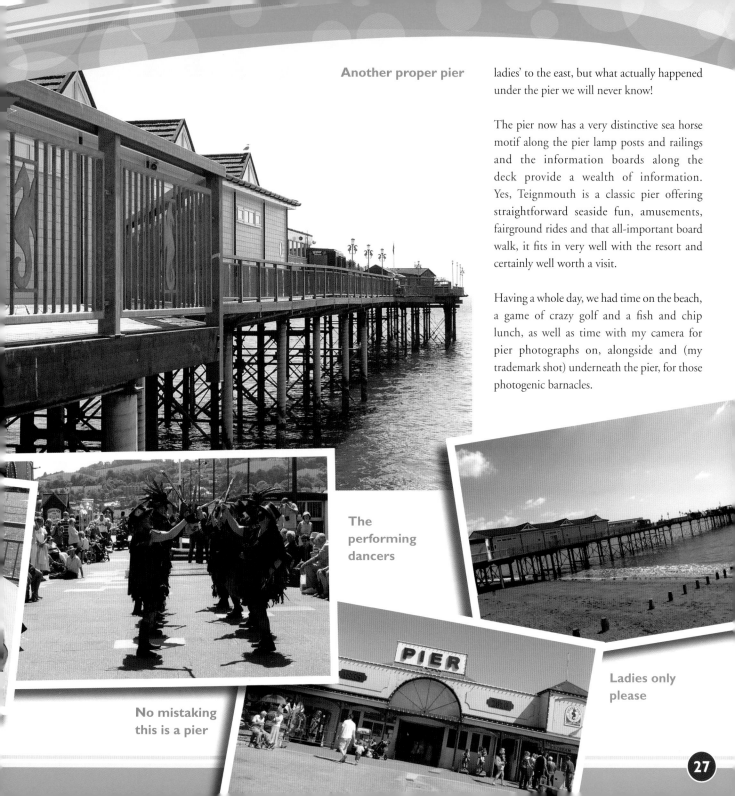

Another proper pier

ladies' to the east, but what actually happened under the pier we will never know!

The pier now has a very distinctive sea horse motif along the pier lamp posts and railings and the information boards along the deck provide a wealth of information. Yes, Teignmouth is a classic pier offering straightforward seaside fun, amusements, fairground rides and that all-important board walk, it fits in very well with the resort and certainly well worth a visit.

Having a whole day, we had time on the beach, a game of crazy golf and a fish and chip lunch, as well as time with my camera for pier photographs on, alongside and (my trademark shot) underneath the pier, for those photogenic barnacles.

The performing dancers

No mistaking this is a pier

Ladies only please

Burnham-on-Sea

We went back to Bridgwater with the family and the following day ventured along the Bristol Channel, where there are supposedly four piers.

First stop: Burnham-on-Sea. Is there really a pier here? Like Torquay, you'd be forgiven for not noticing this one, and when you are aware of Burnham's claim to be home to the UK's shortest pier, you'll understand why.

Short.... it doesn't look like it would reach the sea even at high tide; my facts and figures chart at the end of the book will tell you the actual length, and as you can see from the pics it's certainly not long, but at least it's very easy to walk around for a good selection of photos.

Now on to Weston-Super-Mare, two piers here: The Grand being rebuilt after a catastrophic fire, and the other one a bit of a catastrophe in itself.

Burnham-on-Sea, but the pier isn't

Rides to die for

Weston-Super-Mare
The Grand

It's all brand spanking new

28

Weston-Super -Mare

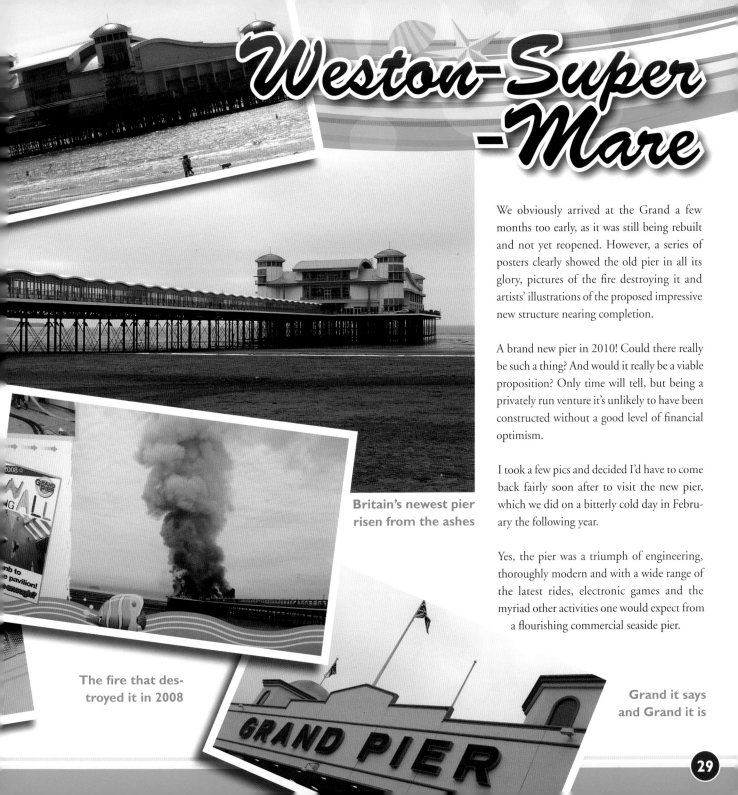

We obviously arrived at the Grand a few months too early, as it was still being rebuilt and not yet reopened. However, a series of posters clearly showed the old pier in all its glory, pictures of the fire destroying it and artists' illustrations of the proposed impressive new structure nearing completion.

A brand new pier in 2010! Could there really be such a thing? And would it really be a viable proposition? Only time will tell, but being a privately run venture it's unlikely to have been constructed without a good level of financial optimism.

I took a few pics and decided I'd have to come back fairly soon after to visit the new pier, which we did on a bitterly cold day in February the following year.

Yes, the pier was a triumph of engineering, thoroughly modern and with a wide range of the latest rides, electronic games and the myriad other activities one would expect from a flourishing commercial seaside pier.

Britain's newest pier risen from the ashes

The fire that destroyed it in 2008

Grand it says and Grand it is

29

Weston-Super-Mare

Some buildings look better than others

One thing we discovered on our second visit and would recommend is the afternoon tea, available in the pier restaurant which really was very, very good.

From the restaurant you also have a good view of the very sorry looking Birnbeck pier a mile up the coast, which was my next port of call.

Birnbeck pier, oh what it must have been like it its heyday? Such an elegant structure but now a very sorry looking pier in a very sorry looking area just to the north of the Grand.

I believe it's unique in having an island in the middle and it's not difficult to imagine how wonderful it could look if restored (which, in today's current economic gloom, looks unlikely), even if there have been numerous plans to develop the site. It looks like the very success of the Grand just down the road, could just be another nail in the Birnbeck's coffin. A real shame.

Mind you the Friends of the Old Birnbeck Pier Society seem to be very active, so you never know!

Birnbeck – So sad

Birnbeck

The decaying buildings on the island

Closing time at Clevedon

Clevedon - sartorial elegance

Pier of the Year 2013

Clevedon

to the officious looking ticket lady and requested a quick walk up and down, but no way was she going to allow any possible out-of-hours pier-walking, even though the pier still had quite a few visitors at the time.

I can assure you, even she couldn't mar a pier visit, especially to one of the most attractive piers I have seen so far. No fun fair, no amusements, just an elegant structure where (for 50p, or whatever it was), you can while away an hour walking over the mouth of the Severn, admiring the views and the workmanship in the pier's construction.

I believe there is a shop in the pagoda-type building at the end, but as we were denied access we couldn't purchase our fridge magnet. We did, however, manage some lovely photos along the pier from an attractive seating area nearby and had it not been for the officious ticket lady, Clevedon would have been my favourite pier to date.

In fact, I'm not the only one that thinks highly of Clevedon, as the pier was voted Pier of the Year 2013 by the NPS membership.

From Clevedon we drove back to Northwood, having completed 7 piers on the 4 day trip and bringing the total up to 17, but we still had 42 to visit so a lot more travelling was still required.

Pictures taken, but sadly no fridge magnet, so we drove up the coast, on a windy non-motorway route to our next pier – Clevedon. I'm pleased to say another success story!

Sadly, whereas we were too early for the Grand in WSM by 2-3 months, we were too late for Clevedon by 5 mins as it closed at 5.00pm and we were there at 5 minutes past. I showed my NPS card

Mumbles

WELCOME TO MUMBLES PIER · CROESO I PIER MWMBWLS

We had a break of two months before our next trip, which was a family gathering in a large house near Llanelli. I was already planning a visit to Mumbles and Penarth and, if all went well, a day trip to Aberystwyth (though that might be a bit of a long shot).

On our first full day (Sunday) I expressed an interest in a visit to Mumbles to see an attractive piece of Welsh coastline... and the pier of course.

So off we ventured late morning to arrive at Mumbles just too late to have been spectators at the annual Mumbles Raft Race. This is a charity event which attracts a very wide variety of seafaring contraptions to race across Swansea Bay. Although we missed the actual race, seeing the exceptionally wide variety of craft, all homemade, come out of the water was an event in itself and we hadn't even arrived at the pier yet.

So onto the pier, quite a commanding structure, with an unusual extra leg, which accommodates the local lifeboat rescue station and launch. This is another pier making a modest charge to visitors, but judging by the condition of parts of the structure on the main pier and the amount of repairs that are no doubt required, the entrance fee would need to be increased somewhat.

Daintily constructed

The amusement rear section looked particularly sad with its discarded, upturned cartoon figure and missing flooring. I wonder whether this section of the pier will eventually be restored to its former glory?

The pier supports also offered an interesting arrangement,

The old lifeboat station

Mumbles overview showing the extra leg

comprising configurations of four pillars and the perimeter enclosure balustrades and infill sections were beautifully ornate. It's amazing how you can easily miss these little details; oh no, I am becoming an anorak.

Currently AMECO (the pier owners), are working with the RNLI to build a new lifeboat station at the pier and convert the existing station to a pier and lifeboat museum.

As I've mentioned, I have also got into the habit of photographing each pier from underneath whenever possible, Jan now regards this as an essential shot in my inventory, but I have been soaked a couple of times by the sea spray – and this was one of them. But an intrepid pier photographer must get his shot.

So off we go back to Llanelli. The story of my mother-in-law being stuck in the lavatory isn't pier-related, so I'll give it a miss.

The rest of our Llanelli holiday was a bit of an anticlimax, well pier-wise certainly. Aberystwyth seemed to be too far for anybody to accompany me on a day trip and Jan fancied stretching out that one for a longer visit. Penarth didn't seem to be well enough placed for a detour on the way back to London, especially with five people and all their luggage on board, so it looks like another pier break was now on the cards.

Work needed at the rear

This cartoon figure's taking a break whilst the repairs take place

Waiting for a cuppa'

Weymouth

Our next planned trip was to Weymouth in November, for two reasons: Number one I don't think either of us had ever been there; and secondly it was a town with two piers.

The first was the bandstand/pier. Well it was a pier and now it's only the front bandstand section. Like Burnham (and similarly constructed) it's very easy to walk around and as far as piers go it's nothing to write home about. Let's hope pier number two has something better to offer.

Well, between the two there are some fine hotel buildings and a delightful clock tower, but the pier... Weymouth Commercial Pleasure pier, isn't that a confusing description? The pavilion is a large monstrous building that didn't even make it in front of the lens.

To the side, there's a passageway headed "Pleasure Pier". I can't think why the approach needed to be so discrete, presumably to allow maximum space for car parking, which seems to be particularly expensive in Weymouth.

The pier bandstand; but where's the rest?

Weymouth Bandstand competing with Burnham for the shortest pier award

Bandstand

The Weymouth Victorian Jubilee Clock tower is much more attractive than the piers

PLEASURE PIER

**Weymouth Pleasure Pier.
Yes that is what it says**

Anyway we marched on and came across the Pavilion cafe, which was closed. Well it was November! I took a few pics and returned. I suppose both these piers had seen better days, but I can't say my pier experience in Weymouth was the best. However, we did find a really good Indian restaurant; a spicy curry always has a calming effect on me.

I revisited Weymouth again in May 2013 and am pleased to say things have improved. The wire fence along the Pleasure Pier passageway has been removed and there's an exciting new pier attraction - the Sea Life Tower. However, the cafe was still closed, the car park was as ugly as ever and the large cumbersome pavilion, though looking better in the summer, still didn't make it in front of the lens

It might have been more pleasurable had the cafe been open at least

May 2013 with the new Sea life Tower in operation

Pleasure Pier

Well I think that's my pier adventure on hold until 2011, but as I now seem to be taking the mission more seriously; maybe I should try and find out a bit more about my subject.

Seaside piers were originally constructed as landing stages for Steam Packet ships, so more visitors could come to the resorts for day trips and bring additional wealth to the areas. The length of the pier was primarily determined by the depth of the sea along that coast. Southend Pier, supposedly the longest in the world, was built that long to allow these steam-driven ships to berth in the shallow Thames Estuary.

The first pier, as we know it, was built in 1814 in Ryde. In total, nearly 100 pleasure piers have existed around the coast of Great Britain of which, as we now know, 59 remain. And for some surviving piers, their days look numbered too.

Finance for these feats of engineering often came from entrepreneurs eager to invest in these structures. Many were also investors in ferry boats and railways, all booming thanks to wealthy Victorians and their growing desire for ozone.

These new piers were soon proving to be tourist attractions in themselves, giving visitors the opportunity to literally walk over the sea, especially in

No shortage of support for Southend

Jolly seating for a rest after the pier walk

Southend pier looking out to sea

Southend-on-Sea

resists with large tidal ranges, where for long periods of the day the sea couldn't even be seen.

As the popularity of piers boomed, so did the amenities offered by these structures over the sea; entertainment; food and drink; theatres; bandstands and pier parties. A pier was becoming an essential part of a seaside town and popular resorts such as Blackpool and Brighton boasted three.

So enough of that stuff - where to next?

A trip to Southend-on-Sea, not very far away, and always good for a day out. But more importantly, it will give us an opportunity to have another look at the world's longest pier.

No visit to Southend would be complete without a walk or train-ride along the pier - all 7080 feet of it - and on this particular day a local breast cancer charity was offering a faux gold medal for completing the 2 ½ mile return trip on foot, so what better incentive.

It is certainly an impressive structure, but you need to visit the pier on a fairly clear day so you can actually see where it ends! Given how far it extends, it is amazing that it remains its full length. From pier to eternity... Good news that the £3 million cultural centre will ensure its future.

With a lifeboat station and visitor centre at the end, a train running along its length and a pier museum (sadly closed that day) there's lots to do and plenty of opportunities for purchasing those elusive fridge magnets.

Including the obligatory fish and chip lunch and a game of crazy golf, as well as another pier to tick off the list, we had a very satisfactory day.

And the view back towards Southend

Let the train take the strain

Sir John Betjeman

The new end-of-the-pier lifeboat station

Swanage

Our next trip was to Dorset for a Groupon offer at the Art Deco Cumberland Hotel in Bournemouth and the opportunity to tick off another three piers. Of course the main reason was a birthday treat for Jan!

Our first port of call was to Swanage, in a lovely position, on the Isle of Purbeck, an area I'd not visited before and which was very nice too.

The pier is an attractive wooden structure with a definite bend in the middle, very ornate railings and sponsored planks. The pier was another one demanding a nominal admission charge, (50p, I think), and I wondered again how far this goes to the pier's upkeep? I've quickly learnt that with piers there's plenty of prohibitively expensive maintenance required! A stark reminder of this fact can be seen by looking at the remaining supports of what could well have been the previous Swanage pier

Swanage; is that a previous Swanage pier alongside?

There's no mistaking that bend

Fancy benches and sponsored decking

running alongside, which did not merit the investment.

Swanage was the NPS Pier of the Year 2012, with a small exhibition centre and museum of local maritime history and memorabilia, where Jan made a friend. There was a very friendly and welcoming atmosphere along the pier (even with a small admission charge). On that bright, sunny day I'm sure Jan could think of no finer way to celebrate her birthday.

Jan found a friend in the Maritime Museum

Sadly, in March 2013 the pier suffered substantial storm damage due to high tides and gale-force winds. Although the damaged section has been temporarily braced, major investment is now required to restore the pier. Local supporters are working hard on a voluntary basis to raise substantial funds by various methods and, in the meantime, the pier is still partially open.

Between them, storm damage, quickly followed by fires and ship collisions, are the blight of most piers and, as you'd expect, are the main reasons for their decline into disuse and, ultimately, closure. Also during the two World Wars, many piers were acquired by the armed forces and were breached to prevent any potential enemy landings. Luckily, most were reinstated after the wars.

Let's hope that Swanage can win its own battle to raise the required funds for its long-term survival.

Classy lighting

Those sponsored planks

Bournemouth

Bournemouth has concrete pillars and a theatre, but for how long?,

We then moved onward to our hotel at Bournemouth, via the chain ferry at Sandbanks (I wonder how many chain ferries there are?) on a brilliantly sunny April day and then on to the pier.

The pier itself is built on substantial concrete supports and there is an open walk-way with a wind-break through to the main pier buildings, which house a substantial theatre and some unusual wavy-styled facades. Underneath there's a mass of concrete pillars, obviously doing their job well, but certainly not as elegant as the decorative metal supports of Clevedon, or even Southend.

Those concrete supports – just plain ugly

It was also lovely to see a bride and groom there posing for photos, I'm assuming the pier was where they first met, or had their first romantic encounter; I bet they were pleased the sun was out and so were we.

I understand that plans are in hand to change the Theatre Pavilion into an adventure sports attraction.

Obviously happy memories for some

Boscombe

Boscombe; Pier of the year 2010. Why??

Tranquillity maybe?

So onward to Boscombe, just along the coast, to another concrete structure, and an ugly one at that! How on earth did Boscombe win a 'Pier of the Year' award? Maybe for peace and tranquillity, as it was closed by the time we arrived, apart from a few licensed fishermen. I didn't think it merited too many shots, so we were quickly on our way.

The pier was almost completely rebuilt in the 1950's, hence the extensive use of concrete, its similarity to a motorway bridge to nowhere, and the unattractive 'bus shelter' type construction along the centre. There had been a theatre at the pier head at some stage which has now been removed, presumably to make way for more fishermen.

As you've probably gathered, Boscombe is not my favourite.

This suited us as I feel I should remind you here that we agreed that the complete pier project was to be carried out amongst holidays, weekends away and visits to friends and family, and not just a whistle-stop pier trip. On these visits my ever-suffering wife, Jan, seemed much more eager to discover places to see that weren't pier-related, so our usual plan was to photograph the pier, get it over with, and then enjoy other local attractions and, of course, a good meal, preferably with bottle of wine.

Anyway, for those of you counting, that now makes 24 to date.

Lowestoft Claremont

Back to our caravan in Suffolk now and up to Lowestoft, another town with two piers, though you'd be forgiven if you thought there was only one when looking along the coast.

Firstly Claremont Pier, a traditional looking pier of wooden construction with an excellent array of amusements at the pier head, including a very busy roller skating rink. Sadly the open air rear section is, like Felixstowe, closed to the public, but we were lucky enough to find an attendant willing to allow us to go outside and take a few shots, even if they did depict a rather sorry scene.

Personally I would call Lowestoft's South Pier a harbour wall, not a pier, what criteria do the NPS use? Like Torquay, there's a lack of supports and apart from the amusement section, this one also appears to be built on dry land. There's nothing there that would convince me I was on a pier.

Well I suppose the big clue is the signage at the front that boldly announces this is The South Pier, though the harbour wall at Whitby looks far more like a pier to me, but it obviously needs a one-arm bandit or two to quality.

In 2000, an artist, David Ward was commissioned by Lowestoft Council to create a visual link between Claremont Pier and South Pier; The "St Elmo's Fire" installation which

Outside work to be done

Lowestoft Claremont - inside fun palace and roller skating rink

was unveiled in 2001 and consists of a group of lights on tall poles, which are reflected on the water between the piers. I couldn't comment on how effective they have been, or whether they still function, but I'll assume not.

Ah well, on to the next one.

St Elmo's lights erected on the Claremont and South Piers to link the pier and 'Harbour Wall'

South Pier

South Pier;
fun at the front

Harwich

Watching our
ship go by

Fishing at
Harwich

Outside - I wouldn't call it a pier!!

This time it's Harwich, a visit we made after a super cruise from Harwich to Iceland and Norway. Called the Halfpenny Pier, because that was the toll charged when it first opened, it was bustling with fishermen and a couple of sunbathers, but not being fond of either activity, it wasn't a 'pleasure' pier to me. Though, realistically, I'm not an amusement man either! As I'm also not over-excited about civil engineering feats, nor a particularly brilliant photographer, I'm now wondering why I'm doing this project in the first place? But never mind, I've started so I'll finish... maybe it should be Mastermind next, with piers as my specialist subject? I think not!

We also passed the pier at the start of our cruise, so the Halfpenny Pier was the first I have managed to photograph from the sea, if that's worth mentioning at all.

I seem to be getting negative thoughts about my quest, so time for another pier trip. Up to north west England, where there are five to savour, to boost my enthusiasm.

Southport

I couldn't bring myself to stay in Blackpool, so stayed at the delightfully named Tickled Trout Hotel, near Preston, on the river Ribble. I did stay there some forty years ago in 1972, when the hotel had only just opened, and a Preston Guild event was on. Lo and behold there was another Preston Guild in 2012. Now this really is a coincidence, because the Preston Guild only takes place every twenty years. The next event is not until 2032, I wonder if my next project will take me there with my zimmer frame?

So now I'm in northern pier country and my first stop is Southport, England's second-longest pier.

A modern elegant-looking pier, but most of the structure appears to be on terra firma, and in spite of it being so long, it only just touches the sea most of the time. We won't worry about such trivia. If the NPS say it's the second-longest, who am I to disagree? But surely it should be measured from the beach at least? Still, not having a tape measure with me I'll take NPS's word for it.

What was good, was to see a pier so obviously successful and in such splendid condition. Being recently refurbished the pier also had a fine selection of plaque sponsors.

There's a lovely traditional penny arcade at the end of the pier, where you can sample the amusements of the past by purchasing and using old pennies; also, a fun land-train is

The penny arcade; remember these?

Southport; looking out to sea... but where is the sea?

Now that's what I call a bench

I think this is the hall of mirrors

St. Anne's

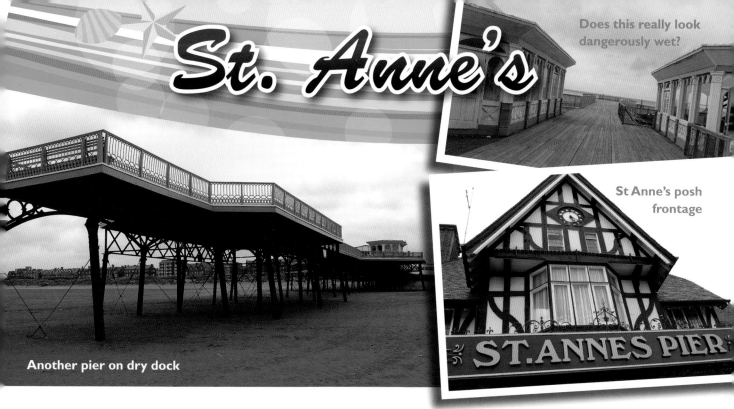

St Anne's posh frontage

ST.ANNES PIER

Another pier on dry dock

provided to ferry you backwards and forwards, and an interestingly designed range of stainless steel street furniture awaits you at the end.

With a large proportion of the pier being over land, it's not quite so easy to see where the parameters of the actual pier buildings start and end, but there are a good selection of amusements, fast food outlets and side shows very close to (if not actually on) the pier, including an old-fashioned hall of mirrors.

Next, to the north west's high-end resort Lytham St Anne's, with a lovely pier, but a less than lovely attendant.

Even the pier head looks posh, modelled on a gabled house, no doubt to blend in with the seaside mansions along the front. No

kiss-me-quick hats here, this is definitely not Blackpool!

We went into the amusement area to walk through to the external section, but were immediately confronted by a less than amiable attendant who told us the pier was closed as the planking was wet, muttering "Health and Safety". This is when I decided to use my NPS card to hopefully gain a concession or two, but our Mr Grumpy wasn't having any of it. The devil in me wanted to sneak through whist Jan kept him busy explaining Health and Safety matters, as she is a dreaded H&S consultant herself, but in the end I settled for a couple of pics through the rear windows... mind you, it didn't look very wet and treacherous to me, mutter mutter...

My signature underneath shots worked out well,

as this was another high and dry pier as the tide was out, so I was fairly satisfied with my range of shots. For posterity, we also took one of Mr Grumpy.

Jan did purchase a fridge magnet, but quite honestly Lytham didn't deserve the custom!

Mr Grumpy – screened to protect the guilty

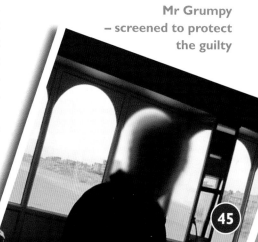

Blackpool
South Pier

Yes, that's Blackpool South

Onward to Blackpool.

The drive along the promenade was much better than I expected. Clean, modern and bright - maybe we should have stayed in "Piertown".

It appears that Blackpool gained from their foray into the Premier League, with supporters from other Premier clubs coming for weekend jaunts and bringing some much needed wealth to the town. Though sadly those days are over. Unfortunately you don't have to travel very far inland before you realise that the promenade is the best part of the town by far.

So, on to the piers and Blackpool is the only town to have three piers. All are in use and at the time they were all owned by Six Piers Ltd; I wonder how accurate the name is?

First the South Pier, I think it's the shortest, constructed with what appears to be far too many metal columns than are actually needed to support the funfair which is the South Pier. Although rusty and decaying in places, the structure still looks OK for a good few years yet. I took a walk around on the sand, as the tide was out and a walk on the pier to confirm that

The big wheel has plenty of support thankfully

I think the pier front hoarding gives a very accurate description of what's inside

Central Pier

Blackpool Central with the its big wheel

Another impressive frontage

Jan and the Blackpool Tower

That's the one; the view below and the storm brewing

Going round in circles to get the right photo

the description on the pier's entrance board, (see photo), is absolutely right.

So that's one completed, now on to pier number two.

Central Pier is the busiest of the three, distinctive because of the dominant big wheel in the centre. Again the big bold frontage gave a very accurate description of what to expect, and again it was absolutely right.

Sadly the famous Blackpool Tower was being refurbished, as it would have given us a seagull's view of all three piers. Instead, for an aerial view we had to venture on to the big wheel, for that all-important Blackpool panorama. Like the South Pier, the Central Pier seems to be faring well. The view from the wheel also afforded us a good insight into the storm that was looming.

Blackpool North Pier

Next, on to the North Pier, the largest Blackpool pier and a very different kettle of fish. Certainly, in my opinion, the best of the three, but unfortunately in need of quite a bit of refurbishment. With a theatre at the end, cafe and bandstand, this pier is definitely aimed at the older generation and actually resembled a more traditional pier. I found out later it was also the oldest of the three. See the information board.

Unlike St Anne's, we were allowed to walk on the very wet decking without incident. Eat your heart out Mr Grumpy! Nice also to see in true English tradition one brave couple sitting outside drinking, presumably, a good English cuppa. Had the sun been shining, with the very ornate seating along the flanks, the scene would have improved no end. However, I really hope it gets the refurbishment it so well deserves and does not end up eclipsed by the other two piers, which are primarily commercial amusement parks on legs.

The view of the North Pier from underneath the Central

Splish splash

The undercover pavilion....really?

Read it for yourself

**Close up
you can see there's
plenty of work needed**

**English cuppa, al fresco,
Blackpool style**

North Pier frontage

So four piers in four days, the most so far; but more importantly, four more to tick off from my list.

I'll also mention that on our return home we drove through Leyland, where there was a parade of vintage commercial vehicles (the name presumably was the clue), and the streets were packed with people enjoying the event. The museum was also worth a visit, if only to see the Pope Mobile - unfortunately he couldn't make it for the procession that day.

Before I move on, I thought I'd mention how the NPS "Pier magazine" has helped to sustain my interest. I'm always pleased to receive the latest copy, even if sometimes it's the only piece of post that comes through the letterbox that I *am* pleased to receive. There's news on all the piers and if it mentions ones I've seen (and the list is rapidly growing), it makes the articles even more meaningful. With nearly 60 (loosely) to feature, there's always news of a restoration (or not) and the extensive library of pictures depicting days of piers gone bye are always worth a look. As a member you are allowed to vote for your best pier for their obviously coveted award. They even have an AGM which I've yet to attend but you never know?

I understand that since my visit, the North Pier has been sold and the new owners - Peter Sedgwick, who own the Big Wheel on the Central pier (how does that work out?) - has plans to restore the pier to its former glory, with a tram running along its length.

Six Piers (if that is what they will still be called), also have plans to update the South and Central Piers, so they all seem to have a future. Blackpool now needs to make a return to the Premier League.

Hythe

The station

Hythe pier simple and effective

The oldest pier train en route to the IOW ferry

I'm sure the rails are straighter than they look here

I had a six month break from piers from July 2011 until February 2012 and our next trip was to Hordle, near Lymington, where there were opportunities to visit four piers on the mainland: Hythe; Southampton; and the two at Southsea; plus perhaps the possibility of a trip to the Isle of Wight, where there were a further four to take in.

It was here where Jan seemed to be putting me under a bit of "pier pressure" as she was of the opinion that a winter holiday break was more important than my pier crusade. We had also inherited a dog, a Cairn terrier called Caesar, so visits to other tourist attractions and long walks seemed to be on the agenda as opposed to pier hopping. So instead of eight we only managed two on this seven-day trip.

The first was Hythe, a good old fashioned working, pleasure pier with its own railway and very much a focal point of this small town. The pier was literally a sponsored plank walkway beside the railway track, along which a very old train ran. Perhaps a cold dank day didn't do much to enhance my experience, but surely this was just a train ride connection to the end of the pier to catch a ferry to the Isle of Wight. So where's the pleasure in that, NPS?

Southampton

Southampton from the IOW ferry, there's no improvement in the view

Southampton from the IOW ferry, there's no improvement in the view

The eyesore that is Southampton Pier

Mind you, it provides an excellent view of vessels large and small going across Southampton Water and the opportunity to ride on the longest surviving pier-train, so maybe I'm being hasty in my criticism.

Unfortunately on this occasion I only had one pier to tick off, though we had agreed to take a visit to Southampton on the way back home to Northwood. Oh dear. Yes Southampton pier? Was it worth including, NPS? Honestly, it's only slightly better than Brighton West and really in a very sorry state. Disused, apart from being a depository for industrial debris, unless, of course, that's actually part of the pier. There is an oriental restaurant on the pier-head, (presumably the pleasure part), which does possibly deserve a visit, but looking over the car queuing lanes for Isle of Wight ferry, it's easy to see this is a pier well past its prime. It's also very unlikely to see any local groups of pier enthusiasts campaigning for the pier's restoration.

We passed Southampton again towards the end of the year on the Isle of Wight ferry - as the photo clearly shows - no change.

Therefore, as far as my pier adventure went this week, my number of piers photographed ended up as one and a half out of a possible eight, so home I go to plan my next trip and I still have 25 piers to tick off, but at least I'm well past the half-way mark.

The Thai Restaurant; does this justify calling it a 'pleasure' pier?

Aberystwyth

North Wales and Anglesey in April 2012 was the next adventure (thanks to a Groupon deal to the north Wales resort of Llandudno). I was determined this trip would be primarily dedicated to my pier mission and my aim was to see all four surviving piers in north Wales and take in the Royal Pier in Aberystwyth too, which had eluded us on the previous Welsh visit.

We left early evening and stayed for a night in Oswestry, at a Premier Inn, en route, before a reasonably early start to take in a very picturesque drive to Aberystwyth. Well, it would have been more picturesque had we not been following a large unattractive white van for most of the journey.

We arrived at Aberystwyth late morning to take the pier photos. The pier was another that seemed to play a central role in the town. The pier head was home to a pub, snooker club and restaurant. Another pier relying on elegant metal supports and significantly shortened over the years. The present owners have left the seaward end of the pier as an outside sun deck which certainly, to me, provides some traditional pier enjoyment.

Aberystwyth - providing night-time entertainment

PRESSURE   Pier Videos   Royal Pier   AMUSEMENTS

The open seating area at the rear for the day-timers

Beaumaris

The popular pastime of crabbing at Beaumaris

Beaumaris Pier - slot machine free

Pics taken, I was ready to head north to the others. Bearing in mind the time it had taken us to get there and somewhat miffed that her desired leisurely stay at Aberystwyth was being rushed, to say the least, Jan wanted to take a look around the town. So that's what we did. The visit included a trip around the centre, a coffee stop, a walk around the castle ruins (no charge) and a look at the funicular railway. Could that be next project? I've just checked; there are only 30 of them, but is there a Funicular Railway Society which I can be critical of ,and a regular magazine? There's also

a camera obscura in Aberystwyth, which might be a project, so we could be back...

Next stop Anglesey, with another stunning drive through north Wales without a white van to follow, then over Robert Stephenson's very impressive dual-function Britannia Bridge to Beaumaris Pier.

Perhaps not the most exciting of piers, but certainly a popular place. I know the sun was shining but there were walkers, crabbers, fishermen and boat-trippers everywhere.

Presumably as they were all pleasurable activities, it certainly seems to have all the attributes of a pleasure pier and without a slot machine in sight. The pier had also recently been refurbished only a month before, which no doubt also had a bearing on its new-found popularity.

But Beaumaris isn't the only pier protruding out into the Menai Strait, as I noticed a far more impressive looking structure on my way to Beaumaris. Indeed, one almost as long as the Strait is wide; Bangor, my next stop.

Bangor

This time I went over Thomas Telford's equally impressive Menai Bridge and arrived at Bangor shortly before closing time at the pier.

Bangor Garth is certainly one of my favourites; elegant, long, in pretty good condition and beautifully architected (if there's such a word) and as it was about to close, very quiet. Grade II listed, the pier has survived its share of problems, including a ship collision and plans for its closure and demolition.

I was particularly taken with the shelters protruding from the main decking, making the whole pier more interesting and pleasing to the eye. The pier's last refurbishment had involved plank sponsorship, a popular and supposedly successful means of fundraising for pier renovations. Apart from the shelters at the end looking a little worse for wear, nothing major

Bangor Pier - stretching across the Menai Strait

The impressive Menai Suspension Bridge

Definitely one of my favourite

Impressive pier entrance gates

seemed to be required. Jan even managed to buy a fridge magnet for the collection after much deliberation, even though the kiosk was attempting to close for the day.

Surprisingly in spite of it being established as one of the most attractive piers surviving today, it has yet to win the NPS Pier of the Year award. I'll vote for it next year!

So now on to the recently refurbished St George's Hotel in Llandudno for a two night stay, leaving the pier until the following morning. The hotel had itself been recently refurbished to its former Victorian glory and afforded very comfortable accommodation.

Very quiet at closing time; fridge magnet shop on right

A loo with a view

Llandudno

The distinctive
Llandudno Pier fork

The following day we toured Llandudno, including the Great Orme, which provided some spectacular pier views and we ventured up to the top in the cable car (which would have been warmer with windows).

The pier seems to be unique as it forks at the end, though its construction isn't too dissimilar to Bangor along the coast with its "outriggers",

if that's what they can be called. However, as you get nearer to the pier you realise that as well as extending towards the sea it also stretches along the coast, supporting a fun fair and amusement section. So much more of a commercial venture than Bangor, it

The
overhead
view from the cable car

The pavilion looks to be in excellent shape

Llandudno out to sea and along the coast

appears to be offering the best of both worlds, with an absolutely delightful pavilion at the end. As with all seaside piers, Llandudno Royal is undergoing a continual renovation programme and parts of this were televised in a recent BBC series. Llandudno, with its impressive pavilions was Pier of the Year in 2005 and is the longest in Wales. Boasting an excellent variety of shops, stalls and amusements, plus of course the opportunity of an 'over the waves' walking experience with some excellent views, Llandudno has something for everyone. Altogether a very satisfactory pier. But...

The view back to land

Good quality decking

Colwyn Bay

Looks better from a distance

Yes, next stop Colwyn Bay's Victoria Pier; a very unsatisfactory state of affairs. Just who would allow such a good-looking work of art to deteriorate to this extent? Sadly, I couldn't get anywhere near the deck because of all the barricading and warning signs, but it really is a very sorry sight.

In fact, the whole area around the pier was in a very run-down state. Has the town given up

Impressive curves

Colwyn Bay:
It must have looked
delightful in its heyday

The sign says it all -
in Welsh as well

But look at
it now

CONWY

ADEILADWAITH
PERYGLUS
CADWCH DRAW
ODDI WRTH Y PIER

DANGEROUS
STRUCTURE
KEEP AWAY
FROM PIER

on tourism? If not, I suggest you don't leave this prominent derelict structure as a focal point. Disappointed of Northwood.

As you'd expect, the current owners (Conwy Council) are hoping for the Heritage Lottery Fund to give them some financial support to restore the pier. We'll wait and see and, in the meantime, no doubt the pier will continue to deteriorate.

On our way home, to make up for disappointment at Colwyn Bay, we stopped off at the Llangollen aqueduct; now that really is worth seeing. You can even walk along the top, if you have a head for heights. Designed by Thomas Telford, clever chap, the 18 towering brick supports took 10 years to build, opening in 1805. I had to include a photo, but how many aqueducts are there and is there an aqueduct club?.... Food for thought....

Now, after completing another five piers in a three-day trip I'm up to 39 with 20 to go, so the 'to do' list is beginning to shorten.

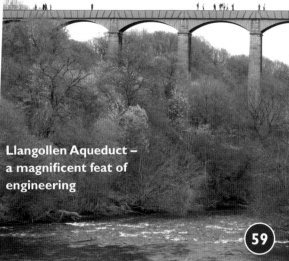

Llangollen Aqueduct –
a magnificent feat of
engineering

Southsea

South Parade
from the sea

If only it can be restored to its former glory

South Parade

South Parade frontage

Our next planned holiday was a Baltic Cruise in May, but leaving from Portsmouth did give me the opportunity to make some visits before and after. Although it might have appeared to be a bit of a rush, I was now on a mission and the project needed to be completed.

So an early start, and heading to Portsmouth, but firstly to Southsea to see the South Parade and Clarence Piers.

The South Parade Pier is certainly impressive! Like many others needing plenty of work (the photographs are deceptive), but it's definitely worthy of restoration. The pavilion was closed and there was a rather dilapidated crazy golf course outside, but a pier that should continue to be.

Since my visit to the pier, concerns had arisen about the lack of investment by its owners, leaving the pier in need of urgent maintenance. Local community groups voted overwhelmingly to support a residents' buy-out, but calls for the council to intervene were rejected and subsequently the pier has now closed. The pier was put up for auction in December 2012 with a reserve price of £210,000, which it didn't achieve.

The price was, no doubt, a snip, but what about those crippling maintenance costs?

But why has Southsea been blessed with two piers?

Clarence

Clarence
underfoot

The sprawl of Clarence –
exposed from the sea

Clarence's
colourful
frontage

After my visit to the Clarence 'Pier', I'm not so sure Southsea has. Unbelievably, it's actually wider than it is long and, to me, it's purely an amusement park on stilts along the beach. Maybe its council tax is reduced because it's not built on completely dry land? I've got to say that I was very thankful to see a number of signs indicating that I was on Clarence pier, or I'd never have fathomed it out.

From the front, the pier head is quite impressive, and you do get a definite feeling there's something better behind. Well, there certainly is!

An adventure playground, arcades, ten-pin bowling, and outdoor fairground attractions including a roller coaster, big wheel and a monster express train. There were also various fast-food outlets, an ice-cream parlour and a posh monogrammed carpet.

So another two piers completed - off to the Baltic.

I'm pleased to say that the cruise also gave me the opportunity to photograph these two piers from the sea, which showed the South Parade Pier in the sun to look very special from a distance, and at the same time portrayed the Clarence pier very much as a fun fair on legs.

Bognor Regis

After St Petersburg...
Bognor Regis. Oh deary deary me

Back from the cruise at the end of May, we returned to London via Bognor Regis, another south coast resort with a pier.

Tourism was late to take off in Bognor, but the resort was chosen as an ideal location for King George V to convalesce during 1929. As a result, the King was asked to bestow the suffix "Regis" on the town. The petition for this was presented to the King's Private Secretary, who in turn delivered it to the King. HRH supposedly replied "Oh, bugger Bognor!" Nevertheless, the message came back to the petitioners as "The King has been graciously pleased to grant your request". A fine example of British diplomacy! I digress again...

I thought I'd remember the pier from my childhood. Well, I didn't remember it as it is now. It's a plain-looking pier and on the pier facia it doesn't even tell you it is a pier, nor what's inside. Is there something more sinister happening? Illicit bingo, or dodgy dodgems perhaps?

And it gets worse

Bognor Regis Pier has had its fair share of disasters. A major storm in the mid sixties sent the far end crashing into the sea and, after a couple of serious fires, it was closed to the public in 1974.

An application for demolition was received soon after and the pier now only survives thanks to the shore-end amusements.

Yes, Bognor is another unloved pier looking for some TLC, it doesn't look attractive and certainly is not particularly pleasurable, though there was one sole fisherman, hopefully having fun.

Oh dear! After all those wonderful palaces in St Petersburg I've come back to Bognor; what more can I say.

Lobster pots and fishing boat in front of the pier

Not forgetting that all important signature shot

The lonely fisherman

The pier with no name

Looks better from further away

Penarth

Another month went by and, after another visit to see my sons and families in Somerset, I popped over to Wales to visit my last Welsh pier - Penarth.

No real complaints with this one, constructed on concrete columns at the pier head and elegant metal supports towards the sea. With an impressive art deco pavilion to which, since my visit, two new zinc domes have been added. The complete structure looked in very reasonable condition and there were plenty of visitors sitting, fishing and promenading on this fine sunny day.

There were lots of seagulls around which gave Caesar plenty to bark at, but the highlight of the day was the fine Italian restaurant just down the road from the pier, the food really was superb and reasonable, and we could sit outside in the sunshine to enjoy it and admire the pier at the same time.

That's all the Welsh piers completed and 43 visited in all, so time to take stock of where to next.

The front could do with a lick of paint

Penarth – a fine pier

Those outriggers again

Another pier with lovely railings

Gravesend

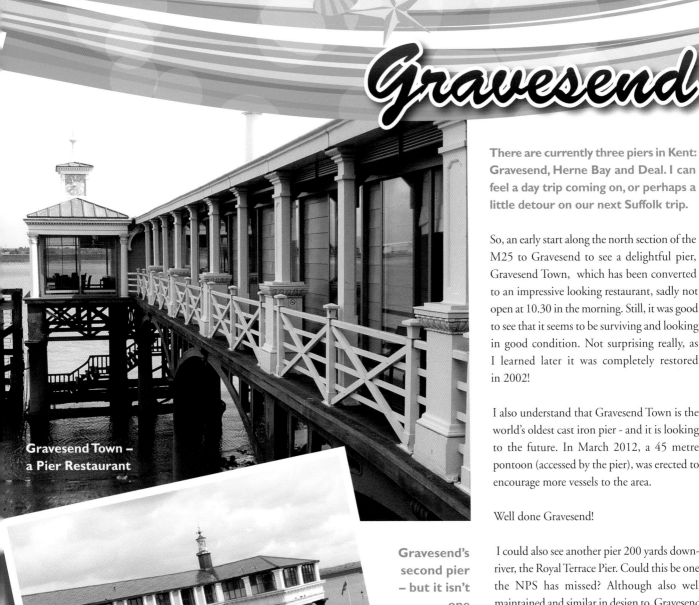

There are currently three piers in Kent: Gravesend, Herne Bay and Deal. I can feel a day trip coming on, or perhaps a little detour on our next Suffolk trip.

So, an early start along the north section of the M25 to Gravesend to see a delightful pier, Gravesend Town, which has been converted to an impressive looking restaurant, sadly not open at 10.30 in the morning. Still, it was good to see that it seems to be surviving and looking in good condition. Not surprising really, as I learned later it was completely restored in 2002!

I also understand that Gravesend Town is the world's oldest cast iron pier - and it is looking to the future. In March 2012, a 45 metre pontoon (accessed by the pier), was erected to encourage more vessels to the area.

Well done Gravesend!

Gravesend Town – a Pier Restaurant

Gravesend's second pier – but it isn't one

I could also see another pier 200 yards down-river, the Royal Terrace Pier. Could this be one the NPS has missed? Although also well maintained and similar in design to Gravesend Town, it doesn't qualify as a pleasure pier as is owned and managed by the Port of London Authority and is therefore classified as a commercial pier... Well, now I know.

Deal

Next stop Deal, where the current concrete pier is the third to be built on the site and I would suggest the least attractive of the three, with a monstrosity of a statue at the pier entrance, though it has an architectural award-winning cafe at the end. I wonder whether it has won any awards for food?

Similar in style to Boscombe, to me it doesn't have the elegance of a metal-columned structure, but is still popular amongst visitors and locals, and particularly with fisherman as the pier is internationally acknowledged as an angling venue.

So much so, that dogs weren't permitted on the pier. This meant that Caesar had to stay with Jan while I did the tour. It had an interesting cafe at the end, which was doing very well that day. Despite Jan's best efforts, Caesar managed to spend the whole 15 minutes I was gone amusing himself by barking at the vast number of seagulls around the pier and had built up quite a rapport with the noise-stricken, delightfully friendly, Pier Master. Before we left, I'm pleased to say, he was still happy to do a photo-call.

Caesar's not good with seagulls...

Detail of the award-winning cafe

Deal – Not the prettiest of piers

The statue at the pier entrance

A pier with a fine outstanding Pier Master

Herne Bay

Herne Bay – a pier of
two halves

Our next stop was a quick to visit some folks in Margate, but these stops are never as quick as you think they are going to be and we were soon behind schedule. We still had to get to Suffolk via Herne Bay! I must admit that Jan did complain a little as this trip was even more of a mad dash than north Wales. However, she did sense that I was on a mission and that in light of my growing fever pitch to get through them, for the time being leisurely weekends were becoming less of an option!

So on to a pit stop visit to Herne Bay, a pier of two halves, not sure where the middle is. The front section of the pier seemed to be surviving well and the surrounding buildings looked quite attractive, but the word 'pleasure' again didn't immediately spring to mind.

And as for the rear section (stranded out to sea) that certainly didn't look in good condition, so it seems as though another major refurbishment project is needed here. Never mind. It was getting late and we still had to get to Suffolk, but at least that was another three off the list, even if there were a few moans and groans attached.

The remains of the Herne Bay pier are actually those of the third pier to be erected on this site and all have suffered from storm and fire damage. Maybe now it's time to call it a day.

Not a particularly good day for fridge magnets either.

Welcome to Herne Bay Pier

Not the most
welcoming

The end bit –
will they ever
meet again

Saltburn-by-the-Sea

Time for another break from piers, but I did manage to acquire a copy of Chris Foote Wood's book 'Walking over the Waves' to find out:

a) The complete project had been completed before

b) And much more comprehensively

c) And in a much shorter time than my three year epic

Chris had also written up every pier he visited with brief history, enhanced with old photos of how each pier used to be in its heyday. So if you are interested in piers, the book is well worth a look. Also, there is an abundance of information on the NPS's web site to satisfy the most avid enthusiast.

Looking through Chris' book, I was horrified to find a mention of a pier at Fleetwood, surely I hadn't left one out on my Blackpool trip, had I? Phew, no I hadn't - it's now demolished, completely, no doubt about it, or it would still be listed by the NPS as a surviving pier, wouldn't it?

Reflecting Saltburn's delicate structure

Jubilee celebrations Saltburn style

My next holiday was to the north east and the lovely fishing-come-tourist village of Staithes, in between Whitby and Redcar. We started our holiday early as my brother (Brian) and wife (Milly) were staying with us for the week and so we thought we'd get the pier bit out of the way before their arrival.

The only pier nearby was Saltburn-by-the-Sea, Yorkshire's only surviving pier, which I made my next port of call on a beautifully sunny Sunday in October. As it was, Saltburn was a delight. An elegant pier amusingly decorated with hand knitted items to commemorate the Queen's Diamond Jubilee earlier in the year, which gave the whole place a carnival atmosphere.

I was prepared for this, as friends are quick to point out to me any news regarding piers. Although I knew of the knitting marathon taking place at Saltburn from a work associate, I was quickly made aware when the event was covered in one of the, all too many, Sunday colour supplements.

THE PIER
ier of the Year 2009

**Saltburn Pier
and cliff lift**

think they have their own pier. Now, I am becoming a knowledgable fellow on the subject, so I explained to our party that this was purely a harbour wall, not a proper pier. But Whitby Corporation, seem to think they are pier owners and if visitors to Whitby enjoy their walks along the the whatever-it-is, then I'm happy for it to be classified as a pleasure pier. But what do I know?

**Caesar strolling under the
pier and there are those
outriggers again**

**Whitby NOT –
a pleasure pier**

To cap it all, alongside the pier was a funicular railway to ferry passengers up and down the cliff. Funicular railways... I wonder....

The sign at the pier head boasts the fact that Saltburn-by-the-Sea was the pier of the year in 2009, when it was presumably last refurbished. It's certainly still looking very good with its simple lines of splayed columns offering little resistance to the waves.

But before I leave Saltburn, I must mention the fish and chip shop along the prom for which, not surprisingly, there was a constant queue for

fish, chips and 'scraps' (the loose bits of batter) all cooked in good northern dripping, with an optional accompaniement of a generous ladle of curry sauce to provide an international flavour. Being Southerners, we stuck to the standard cod and chips and then felt extreme pangs of guilt for overdoing the cholestoral; they were delicious!

The remainder of the week was pier-free, but on a day trip to Whitby we discovered that they

Cleethorpes

Now the journey back home from Staithes, and potentially three piers to see: Cleethorpes; Skegness and (with a very early start and a late end to the journey), maybe even Cromer. However, there was one major flaw in the plan as we had to be home in time to be poshed-up for a friend's birthday party at the golf club by eight. Therefore Cromer was scrapped off the schedule to my wife's delight (with a more leisurely stay in that area in mind...)

One thing you find when pier trekking is that you often travel along routes you'd never normally use - an experience in itself - and this journey included a trip over the Humber Bridge. I believe at one time, the world's longest suspension bridge. Now, I wonder how many suspension bridges there are in the UK and if there's a suspension bridge appreciation society...?

So onto Cleethorpes, a place I'd never been to before, and not one I'd be particularly eager to return to. And the pier was closed. This was certainly a pleasure pier until quite recently, so we parked the car and headed for the pier, only to encounter a tremendous hail storm. Wow, it actually stung us and Caesar didn't know what had hit him, numerous times. We took refuge over a cup of tea, the storm soon subsided and the photos were duly taken.

Like many others, the future of Cleethorpes pier is uncertain. The last owners spent a great deal of money converting it to a night club, but now it is once again for sale. So if you're interested in what happens next, take a look at the NPS's web site links.

Cleethorpes - supposedly massive plans on the cards

It's those donkeys again

Skegness

Now onto Skegness. I was last in Skegness nearly 50 years ago, at the Butlin's holiday camp, as part of a group of expectant teenagers on their first holiday without their parents. Good morning campers etc.

This though, was an altogether more serious visit. Skegness pier is like Southport, it's hard to see where the pier actually starts, but there is a proper pier at the end at least with all the traditional attributes one would expect.

Skegness is a lively resort and the pier complements this well, and once you've managed to get through the commercial three quarters, there is somewhere to promenade and sit, in a no doubt very bracing easterly wind. Nice enough I suppose, but I've got to say not my cup of tea really, so back home to that party in Pinner.

So that's now 49 piers visited, or viewed at least with just ten to go and four of them are on the Isle of Wight, so that's obviously where I should be going next.

Skegness – the pier end, shame about the rest!

Skegness - the amusements at the shore end

It's a proper pier at the sea end

Ryde

The Isle of Wight in its heyday was home to eleven piers, but sadly only four now remain: Ryde; Sandown; Totland Bay and Yarmouth.

We booked the very comfortable Melbourne Hotel in Shanklin, as it accepted dogs; Caesar had become an active pier-spotter now, though pier-piddler might be a more appropriate term.

So a November weekend on the IOW, at least we'd miss the crowds, though I do have to say I was impressed with the island out of season. The ferry from Southampton also gave me the opportunity to take some sea-side photos of Southampton Pier, but it didn't make it look any better I'm afraid.

We sat in the special outdoor sheltered doggy lounge on the ferry. Supposedly the Solent is one of the most expensive pieces of water in the world to ferry across. On to Ryde; which I'd categorise as a 'commercial working pleasure' pier, like Weymouth.

This was definitely something different, for although Hythe on the mainland also transported passengers by train to meet the ferries, Ryde used retired London Underground Bakerloo Line rolling stock carriages, which I remembered well. Ryde was also the first pier I had come across that allowed cars, in fact quite a large area was devoted to car parking, and I thought it was only in the USA they did this.

Reliable vintage London Underground stock

Gosh a pier with a car park, I simply don't believe it

Festive bunting in the booking hall

Not an attractive pier

Sandown

The pier also had a wide curve and was functional rather than attractive, but the side rails were decorative and the booking office exterior was not unpleasant. The pier's commercial side would hopefully ensure its future and a maintenance and repair pro-gramme was obviously in full flow. By the way, I'm assuming the pleasure bit was the cafe in the booking office at the end!

We thought we'd visit Sandown next, on the way to Shanklin,. A proper pleasure pier, with amusements and bright lights. Sadly, the open air end section was closed when we arrived but the pier's slogan 'A whole day's Fun in One' I'm pretty sure holds true. So far the piers on the IOW have proved to be one commercial-ish and one fun palace, what would the other two bring?

Sandown Pier by day

Sandown pier by night

It is no doubt what it says it is

Totland Bay

Why would you want to enter?

The following day we visited Totland bay and Yarmouth, so we'd have day three for Osborne House, a 'must'. Plus, of course, a long dog walk, also now a must.

Totland Bay first then. I'm afraid it's one of those sad and sorry sights I've now become accustomed to on my pier mission. Not sure why it was actually built where it is, it's hardly a resort. But if there were eleven piers on the island, I'm assuming there must have been a demand at some stage.

I real pity, as I liked the pier's ninety degree turn at the end and the view down on to the pier from the top of the headland. I won't mention Jan's fall in her quest to try and outdo me with her own photo reportage! Still, the pictures tell the story well; the pier is very much in need of a rebuild and that is another project that's very unlikely to take place in today's economic times, especially as Totland bay is in such a quiet part of the island. So if you want to see this pier, I feel it's one to visit sooner rather than later as I don't know how much longer it will be there.

Now on to Yarmouth, just along the coast from Totland, with a pier that had a very different feel to it. What appealed to me most was the village feel that Yarmouth had; a few interesting shops complemented with tea rooms and a small hotel, and once again the pier was the main focal point of the village.

The view from the cliff top

Totland Bay – its days are certainly numbered

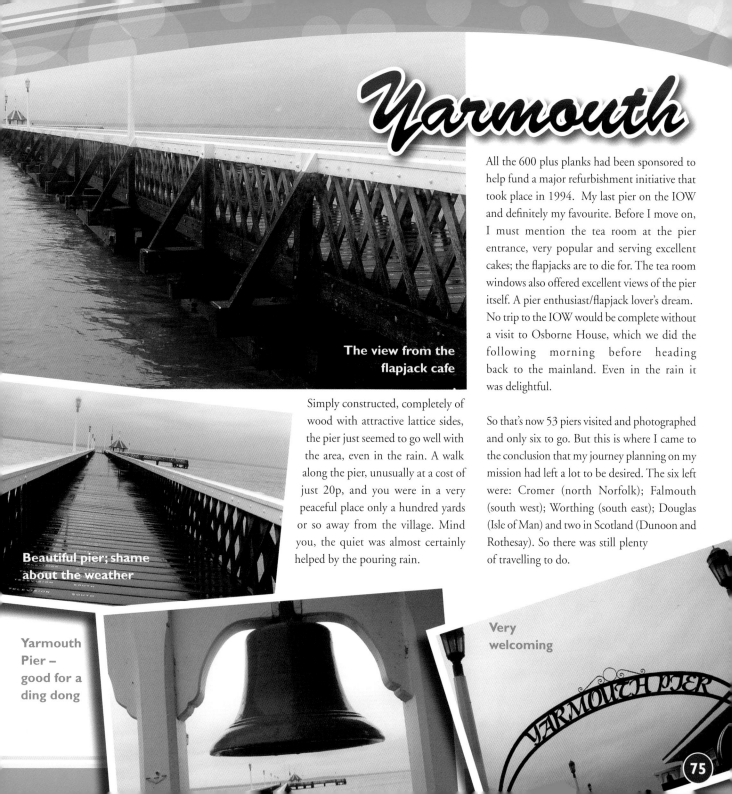

Yarmouth

All the 600 plus planks had been sponsored to help fund a major refurbishment initiative that took place in 1994. My last pier on the IOW and definitely my favourite. Before I move on, I must mention the tea room at the pier entrance, very popular and serving excellent cakes; the flapjacks are to die for. The tea room windows also offered excellent views of the pier itself. A pier enthusiast/flapjack lover's dream. No trip to the IOW would be complete without a visit to Osborne House, which we did the following morning before heading back to the mainland. Even in the rain it was delightful.

So that's now 53 piers visited and photographed and only six to go. But this is where I came to the conclusion that my journey planning on my mission had left a lot to be desired. The six left were: Cromer (north Norfolk); Falmouth (south west); Worthing (south east); Douglas (Isle of Man) and two in Scotland (Dunoon and Rothesay). So there was still plenty of travelling to do.

The view from the flapjack cafe

Simply constructed, completely of wood with attractive lattice sides, the pier just seemed to go well with the area, even in the rain. A walk along the pier, unusually at a cost of just 20p, and you were in a very peaceful place only a hundred yards or so away from the village. Mind you, the quiet was almost certainly helped by the pouring rain.

Beautiful pier; shame about the weather

Yarmouth Pier – good for a ding dong

Very welcoming

Worthing

A winter sunset at Worthing

Of the remaining piers, there was only one left that could realistically be completed in a day trip and that was Worthing. Once again, I felt it was time we took the in-laws (Sheila and Les) out for another day at the seaside, and the 4th December was also the day after Les's birthday, so he was due a real treat.

The weather was fairly kind to us, and their Blue Badge got us parked centrally in town for the shops and the pier, very useful when there are crowds of Christmas shoppers for a wheelchair to negotiate. How could I not have been to Worthing pier before? It's another proper south coast pier along the lines of Eastbourne and Brighton and a splendid example.

Another proper pier on the south coast

Looking back to the town

Worthing has fishermen too

Pier of the Year 2006

76

Boat leaving Falmouth Pier

Falmouth

The view from M&S

The distinctive pier buildings and theatre were all doing well and the short December day gave me the opportunity to take some sunset shots, I'm becoming a bit of a professional at last.

Fish and chips in a nearby cafe, followed by a cream tea in the pier tea rooms; truly a day for my father-in-law to remember.

Fridge magnet duly purchased; another pier ticked off!

Next we booked an early December trip to Mevagissey using a good old Groupon deal (my wife's addicted to them), to the delightful Trevalso Court hotel overlooking Mevagissey Bay. The setting was really stunning and Cornwall (without the summer traffic jams getting there, and the crowds once you are there), is really a lovely place. And the weather was great, given the time of year. We arrived early evening and the next day we ventured to Falmouth, via King Harry's Ferry and some very minor roads.

Falmouth is hardly the most stunning pier in the UK, but it is a pier, (that's if you don't mistake it for a jetty). It is well-used, in reasonable condition and if NPS say it's a pier, it's a pier. But whether it's worth a 500 mile return trip to Cornwall is debateable.

The pier cafe was closed when we visited in December, but we did manage to have a stop at the Marks and Spencer cafe which looks out onto the harbour directly over the pier. Thank you for that tip Mr Foote Wood.

Pier completed, we spent the next day at a very quiet Eden Project, another day with glorious sunshine and then back home with only four piers now to visit.

Cromer

The view from above

The next trip was to Cromer for another week's holiday with Brian and Milly. A whole week away and only one pier, this fitted in much more with Jan's ideas of a pier crusade. We stayed in a cottage high on the cliffs at Overstrand, a very scenic mile's walk along the coast to Cromer and I'm so pleased to report that Cromer is another attractive and successful pier. And seven days to take photographs of it!

Cromer from below... oops, drenched again

Being off season, as most of my trips were, I was pleased to see the pier was going through some major repairs which I now know is a very expensive (1.2 million pounds worth) and specialised job.

The pier itself is an attractive Art Deco affair and in addition to the sweeping steps at the pier head and mosaic compass, there was also a thriving theatre and lifeboat exhibition at the end of the pier. January isn't the peak of the holiday season in Cromer, so unfortunately the theatre would not be opening again until March. I will admit to you that Cromer was one of the occasions I managed to get drenched taking one of my signature underneath-the-pier shots.

So just three more piers. Do I really need to go to the Isle of Man? After all, the pier at Ramsey has been closed for years, it's a long way and for what? I mentioned this to my eldest son on the phone and he was outraged

that I could even contemplate leaving a pier out, so I was shamed into it.

I was considering a quick flight to the IOM, a bus up to Ramsey, a couple of quick pics then back home. But that did seem a very expensive exercise, and quite honestly I think Jan wanted to see all the piers too really. Oh, why didn't

Business as usual for the pier maintenance team

Ramsey

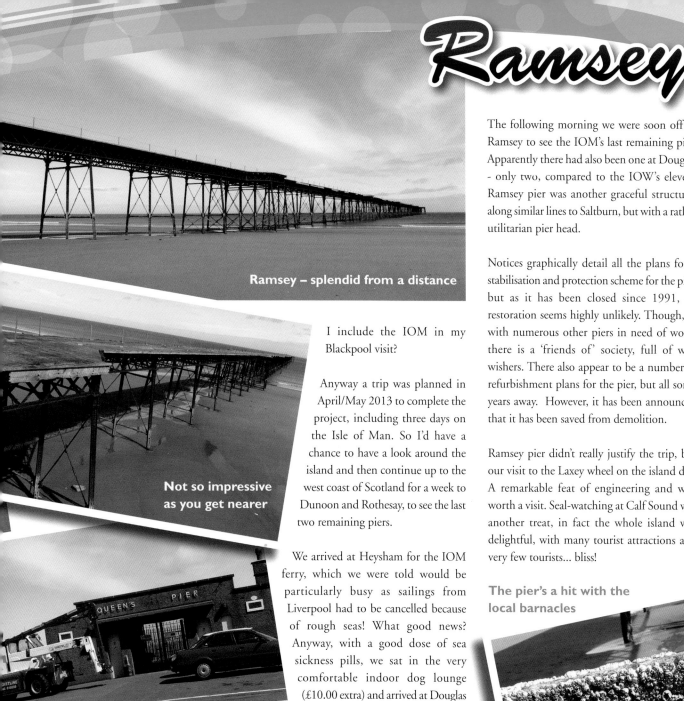

Ramsey – splendid from a distance

Not so impressive as you get nearer

Could work be about to start?

The following morning we were soon off to Ramsey to see the IOM's last remaining pier. Apparently there had also been one at Douglas - only two, compared to the IOW's eleven. Ramsey pier was another graceful structure, along similar lines to Saltburn, but with a rather utilitarian pier head.

Notices graphically detail all the plans for a stabilisation and protection scheme for the pier, but as it has been closed since 1991, its restoration seems highly unlikely. Though, as with numerous other piers in need of work, there is a 'friends of' society, full of well wishers. There also appear to be a number of refurbishment plans for the pier, but all some years away. However, it has been announced that it has been saved from demolition.

Ramsey pier didn't really justify the trip, but our visit to the Laxey wheel on the island did. A remarkable feat of engineering and well worth a visit. Seal-watching at Calf Sound was another treat, in fact the whole island was delightful, with many tourist attractions and very few tourists... bliss!

I include the IOM in my Blackpool visit?

Anyway a trip was planned in April/May 2013 to complete the project, including three days on the Isle of Man. So I'd have a chance to have a look around the island and then continue up to the west coast of Scotland for a week to Dunoon and Rothesay, to see the last two remaining piers.

We arrived at Heysham for the IOM ferry, which we were told would be particularly busy as sailings from Liverpool had to be cancelled because of rough seas! What good news? Anyway, with a good dose of sea sickness pills, we sat in the very comfortable indoor dog lounge (£10.00 extra) and arrived at Douglas at 6.00pm, shaken but not stirred.

The pier's a hit with the local barnacles

Dunoon

So now the ferry back to Heysham, (in much calmer waters) and on to the Cowal Peninsular and the only two remaining piers in Scotland. Via another very expensive ferry from Gourock to Dunoon.

Dunoon is yet another pier that is closed to the public. A real shame, as it's a very attractive building, but sadly now in a poor state of repair. I had only just started taking a few photos before an elderly resident handed me a black and white copy of how the pier looked in its heyday, which, when he knew of my mission, he insisted I kept.

The pier has been closed now for over two years and foot-ferry passengers currently use a far less attractive jetty 50 yards further down the Clyde. But if you are crossing by car like we were, the disembarkation point is now at Hunters Quay, a mile to the north of Dunoon. During our week we stayed at Inellen, a Clydeside village 3 miles south of Dunoon in a lovely apartment overlooking the estuary. Whilst there we learned a great deal about the passions of the locals who seemed to have two main topics of conversation: the cost and number of companies operating the ferries across the Clyde; and how much they would like to see their beloved pier restored.

The pier urgently needs some restoration work

Dunoon Pier – the talk of the town

Who's that!!

Strictly No Unauthorised Entry

I also learnt that the Waverley, the last remaining passenger steam ship, makes frequent visits to Dunoon in the summer, presumably because of its pier traditions. I should definitely plan to make a steam ship voyage on the Waverley at some stage; maybe once the pier has been reopened. Also If I decided that my next project was to be surviving passenger steam ships (is there a society?), it could be completed in a day!

But will the Waverley ever berth at Dunoon Pier again?

On one of our days in Dunoon I was lucky enough to be escorted along the pier by a representative of Calmag Ferries (the current owners), another resident who was passionate about the pier's restoration. By the way, I thought I'd mention that it wasn't me clambering over the pier fence to take a closer look.

What I would say is that whether or not you are a pier enthusiast, this part of Scotland is really beautiful, still relatively unspoilt and very well worth a visit.

So just one more to go!

Looking across the Cowal peninsular from the statue of Robert Burns' love Highland Mary.

Rothesay

They say leave the best until last. Well, I certainly didn't achieve that, though the drive to Colintraive was exceptional, even if it was only to get another prohibitively expensive ferry to Bute.

Onward to Rothesay, a modern looking building on a pier that was actually open and in use. The original pier burnt down some years ago, but the present building (which is basically only a booking office) has been modelled on the original, and was opened by the Queen Mother.

But maybe it was the dull drizzly day, or I was just expecting more of a finale, but I really was hoping my final pier would have more to offer. It was along similar lines to Dunoon but although styled on the old building (as we could see from the photographs in the lovely Victorian building now being used as a Tourist Information Centre), it just seemed to lack the feel of a pier. Even though there was a ferry loading and unloading whilst we were there.

We did take advantage of the picturesque Victorian conveniences nearby, resplendent with original tiles and glass cisterns, well worth 20p. After which we journeyed on to Mount Stuart House and Gardens which turned out to be the highlight of our day in Bute.

Rothesay Pavilion – another disappointment

Rothesay Pier or glorified booking office

What Next?

59 piers and 59 piers ticked off: Project complete!

So my adventure is finally over. Although, when I first started my photographic crusade I wasn't really sure why I was doing it, my interest in piers has definitely developed throughout my journey. I am now always keen to find out still more about these delightful coastal landmarks majestically stretching out to sea (or not), especially now that I have visited them all in all their glory. So yes, it's official, I am now an anorak!

I will still remain a member of the National Piers Society and eagerly read news about our seaside piers, even though it is generally focussed around doom and gloom. Friends and family will no doubt continue to feed me any pier information and articles, with questions like "They are always coming up for sale,

why don't you buy one?" The answer to that is a very firm "never!!!" But I know I will always feel affectionate towards them.

For anybody wondering about my next adventure, I'm afraid I don't have any more projects planned, at the moment. Secretly, I think Jan is hoping that, instead of visiting decaying and rusting sea monoliths, I will start a new odyssey, so that we can set off around the country (or world? She's thinking big!), for our future holidays...

Mind you, having a conversation with one of my friend's wives at the golf club a few months ago, we seemed to be at crossed-purposes and it was several minutes before I realised that I was talking about piers, whilst she thought I was waxing lyrical about beers!!!! Well now, that really might well be a project opportunity....

Victorian opulence

Ornate wash basins to match

Where are the Piers

Map Key

The Surviving Piers

Pier	Page	Date Visited	Date Opened	Designer	Original Length	Current Length	Current Owners	Fridge Magnet	Comment
Aberystwyth Royal	52	11.04.12	1865	Eugenius Birch	212M	91M Dom	Leisure	YES	A pier of two halves for day and night
Bangor Garth	54	11.04.12	1893	John James Webster	472M	458M	Bangor Council	YES	One of my favourites and outriggers too
Beaumaris	53	11.04.12	1846	Frederick Foster	174M	174M	Isle of Anglesey Council	YES	Refurbished March 2012- a popular local attraction
Blackpool Central	47	08.07.11	1868	J I Mawson	463M	341M	Six Piers	YES	The dominent big wheel was added in 1990
Blackpool North (current)	48	08.07.11	1863	Eugenius Birch	430M	402M	Peter Sedgewick	YES	Major refurbishment to be started and a tram as well
Blackpool South	46	08.07.11	1893	T Worthington & J Harker	150M	150M	Six Piers	YES	A real Blackpool Pleasure Pier
Bognor Regis	62	26.05.12	1865	Sir Charles Fox & Joseph Wilson	305M	107M	Bognor Regis Leisure	YES	Not one to visit after St Petersburg
Boscombe	41	11.04.11	1889	Archibald Smith	183M	229M	Bournemouth Corporation	NO	Wouldn't have been my Pier of the Year
Bournemouth	40	10.04.11	1856	Eugenius Birch	305M	229M	Bournemouth Corporation	YES	Looks better from above
Brighton Palace	20	13.06.10	1899	Richard St George Moore	537M	537M	The Noble Organisation	YES	The most visited pier in the UK
Brighton West	21	13.06.10	1866	Eugenius Birch	340M	n/a	Brighton West Pier trust	NO	Site of the world's first vertical pier?
Burnham-on-Sea	28	21.06.10	1914	Unknown	37M	37M	The Parkin Family	YES	The shortest UK pier; or is it?
Clacton-on-Sea	16	24.05.10	1871	Peter Bruff	146M	360M	The Clacton Pier Company	YES	All the fun of the fair
Cleethorpes Pier 39	70	27.10.12	1873	J E and A Dowson	366M	102M	Peacefields Properties	NO	Currently up for sale, a snip at £400,000
Clevedon	31	21.06.10	1869	R Ward & J Glover	257M	257M	Clevedon Pier & Heritage Trust	NO	Sartorial elegance
Colwyn Bay Victoria	58	13.04.12	1900	Maynell& Littlewood	67M	229M	Conwy C B C	NO	Pull it down
Cromer	78	06.01.13	1901	Douglass& Arnott	153M	153M	North Norfolk DC	YES	A fine example
Deal (current)	66	07.07.12	1957	Sir W Halcrow and Partners	313M	313M	Dover District Council	YES	Stylish for concrete I suppose
Dunoon	80	20.04.13	1835	Unknown	130M	130M	Argyle & Bute Council	YES	Definitely worthy of refurbishment
Eastbourne	8	21.11.09	1870	Eugenius Birch	305M	305M	Six Piers	NO	Where it all started
Falmouth	77	10.12.12	1905	W Tresidder	155M	155M	Carrick CC	YES	A solid working pier
Felixstowe	18	29.05.10	1905	Unknown	805M	136M	Pier Amusements Ltd	YES	Futuristic plans have been approved. So there's hope
Gravesend Town	65	07.07.12	1834	W Clark	79M	79M	Gravesend Borough Council	NO	The world's oldest cast iron pier and doing well
Gt. Yarmouth Brittania	12	01.04.10	1902	J & A Mayoh	168M	168M	Family Amusements Ltd	NO	In spite of problems in the past, surviving well
Gt. Yarmouth Wellington	13	01.04.10	1853	P Ashcroft	212M	150M?	Family amusements Ltd	NO	Bowling alley over the sand
Harwich Halfpenny	43	15.06.11	1853	P Bruff	105M	60M	Harwich Haven Authority	NO	Fisherman's friend
Hastings	10	22.11.09	1872	Eugenius Birch	278M	278M	Hastings Pier & White Rock Trust.	NO	Can it really be saved?

Name	No.	Date	Year	Engineer	Length 1	Length 2	Owner	Open	Description
erne Bay (current)	67	07.07.12	1899	Wilkinson & Smith	1155M	98M	Canterbury county Council	NO	A pier of two halves
ythe	50	13.02.12	1878	J Wright	640M	640M	White Horse Ferries	YES	Good for a train ride to the Isle of Wight
andudno	56	12.04.12	1877	J Brunlees	700M	700M	Six Piers Ltd	YES	The pier that has everything
owestoft Claremont	42	23.04.11	1903	D Fox	230M	220M	David Scott & Family	YES	Success at the front but work needed at the rear & up for sale
owestoft South	43	23.04.11	1846	Sir Morton Peto	403M	403M	Oulton Broad Leisure	YES	Pier or harbour wall? That is the question
umbles	32	15.08.10	1898	W Marsh	255M	255M	Ameco Ltd	YES	Joint venture to develop the pier should secure its futureX
aignton	24	18.06.10	1879	G Bridgman	238M	226M	U K Piers Ltd	YES	Typical seaside pier just enough of everything
enarth	64	25.06.12	1896	H Edwards	200M	200M	Vale of Glamorgan D C	YES	Wonderful pier with a fine Art Deco pavilion
amsey Queens IOM	82	18.04.13	1886	Sir John Good	684M	684M	I O M Government	YES	Restoration-wise - many plans, but little money
othesey Bute	82	22.04.13	1890	n/a	n/a	n/a	Isle of Bute	YES	A ferry terminal and booking office
yde IOW	72	19.1.12	1814	J Kent	530M	703M	Wight Link ltd	YES	The London Underground goes to the IOW
t Anne's	45	08.07.11	1898	W Marsh	280M	183M	Clark Leisure catering	YES	Don't go if there's the sightest hint of precipitation
altburn-by-the-Sea	68	21.10.12	1869	J Anderson	458M	206M	Redcar and Cleveland B C	YES	Pier and Funicular Tramway both delightful
andown Culver IOW	73	19.11.12	1879	T Saunders	297M	297M	Sandown Pier Leisure	YES	"A Whole Day's Fun in One"
kegness	71	27.10.12	1881	C Clarke & R Pickwell	554M	118M	UK Piers Ltd	YES	Colourful and Commercial
outhampton Royal	51	18.02.12	1833	n/a	275M	275M	Red Funnel	NO	"Oh dear, oh dear, oh dear"
outhend-on-Sea	36	27.03.11	1829	J Brunlees	2195M	2195M	Southend-on-Sea BC	YES	The world's longest pleasure pier
outhport	44	07.07.11	1860	J Brunlees	1090M	1108M	Sefton BC	YES	The UK's second longest pier
outhsea Clarence	61	11.05.12	1861	Mouchel and Ptnrs	40M	40M	Southses Clarence Pier Co	YES	A funfair on the beach
outhsea South Parade	60	11.05.12	1908	G Smith	300M	183M	Six Piers	YES	Uncertain future for a traditional seaside pier still up for sale
outhwold	14	29.04.10	1900	B Howard	245M	190M	Stephen Bourne	YES	A pier success story on the East Anglian coast
wanage	38	10.04.11	1859	J Walton	227M	196M	Swanage Pier Trust	YES	A charming, well cared for traditional seaside pier
eignmouth Grand	26	20.06.10	1867	J Wilson	214M	191M	Grand Pier Teighmouth Ltd	YES	A traditional all-family seaside pleasure pier
orquay Princess	22	19.06.10	1894	A Thorne	238M	238M	Torbay CC	YES	A nice stroll to chat to the fishermen
otland Bay IOW	74	20.11.12	1880	S & S Yockney	137M	137M	Derek Barren	NO	A lovely pier but very unlikely to be saved
Walton-on-the-Naze	17	24.05.10	1830	P Bruff	244M	793M	New Walton Pier Co	YES	The focal point of the town
Veston-Super-Mare Birkbeck	29	21.06.10	1867	Eugenius Birch	346M	317M	Urban Splash	NO	A derelict pier with an island but one well worth saving
Veston-Super-Mare Grand	28	21.06.10	1904	A Meek	327M	366M	Grand Pier ltd	YES	Rebuilt after the fire in 2008. One of the UK's premier piers
Veymouth Bandstand	34	07.11.10	1938	V Venning	61M	16M	Weymouth & Portland BC	YES	Now an Art Deco beach bandstand but not really a pier
Veymouth Commercial	35	07.11.10	1933	n/a	273M	297M	Weymouth & Portland BC	NO	A commerial pleasure pier and not one of my favourites
Vorthing	76	02.12.12	1862	Sir Robert Rawlinson	292M	300M	Worthing BC	YES	Traditional south coast Art Deco pier - a treasure
armouth IOW	75	20.11.12	1876	Denham 7 Jenvey	209M	186M	Yarmouth Harbour Commissioners		A delightful wooden pier; a definite favoirite

The Lost Piers

Lost Piers	Length approx	Year Opened	Year Lost	Remarks
Aberavon	275M	1898	1962	Only a length of rusty iron railing remains
Aldburgh	75M	1878	1909	Hit by a vessel during construction and never completed
Alum Bay(IOW)	120M	1869	1958	Damaged in 1927 and never repaired
Brighton Chain	345M	1823	1896	Storm damage, neglect and competition from other piers led to its demise
Coatham	550M	1875	1899	Storm damage. Pavilion is now a cinema
Cowes Royal (IOW)	75M	1867	1882	Storm in 1876 damaged the pier beyond repair
Cowes Victoria (IOW)	50M	1902	1961	Fire damage after WW2 and never repaired
Douglas (IOM)	n/a	1869	1894	Closed by the council and sold for scrap
Dover Promenade	275M	1893	1927	Extensive building work required made repair unviable
Fleetwood Victoria	150M	1910	2008	Series of fires between 1952 and 2008 lead to demolition
Folkstone Victoria	210M	1888	1954	Sectioned for defence 1940 but fire 1943 lead to later demolition
Hornsea	325M	1880	1897	Various disputes/financial problems and a ship collision assisted its demise
Hunstanton	250M	1870	1978	In its heyday it sported a zoo, but a storm destroyed most of it in 1978. Arguably East Anglia's finest pier
Lee on Solent	225M	1888	1958	Damaged in WW2, the compensation received was spent elsewhere
Leith Trinity Chain	190M	1821	1898	An interesting chain pier, it fell into disuse when harbours in the vicinity were improved, and was eventually irreparably damaged by a storm.
Lytham	275M	1865	1960	Fire and ship damage meant it was closed in 1938 and it was eventually demolished.
Margate	300M	1855	1978	The first iron pier, really a jetty it was closed in 1976 on safety grounds, though part of the pier head still survives.
Minehead	210M	1901	1940	Completely demolished during WW2. Plans to rebuild the pier never came to fruition.
Morcambe Central	280M	1869	1992	Destroyed by fire, it was condemned in 1991 with demolition soon after.
Morcambe West End	545M	1896	1978	Plagued by storm-damage and prohibitive repair costs which lead to demolition. Plans for a new pier never materialised.

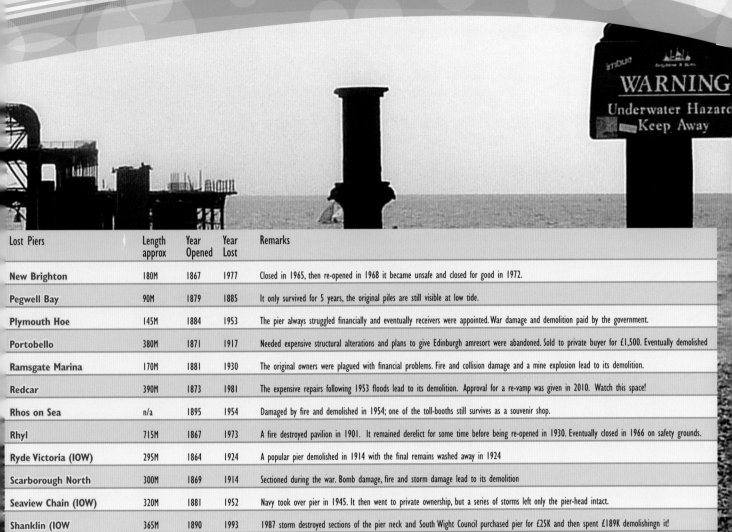

WARNING
Underwater Hazard
Keep Away

Lost Piers	Length approx	Year Opened	Year Lost	Remarks
New Brighton	180M	1867	1977	Closed in 1965, then re-opened in 1968 it became unsafe and closed for good in 1972.
Pegwell Bay	90M	1879	1885	It only survived for 5 years, the original piles are still visible at low tide.
Plymouth Hoe	145M	1884	1953	The pier always struggled financially and eventually receivers were appointed. War damage and demolition paid by the government.
Portobello	380M	1871	1917	Needed expensive structural alterations and plans to give Edinburgh amresort were abandoned. Sold to private buyer for £1,500. Eventually demolished
Ramsgate Marina	170M	1881	1930	The original owners were plagued with financial problems. Fire and collision damage and a mine explosion lead to its demolition.
Redcar	390M	1873	1981	The expensive repairs following 1953 floods lead to its demolition. Approval for a re-vamp was given in 2010. Watch this space!
Rhos on Sea	n/a	1895	1954	Damaged by fire and demolished in 1954; one of the toll-booths still survives as a souvenir shop.
Rhyl	715M	1867	1973	A fire destroyed pavilion in 1901. It remained derelict for some time before being re-opened in 1930. Eventually closed in 1966 on safety grounds.
Ryde Victoria (IOW)	295M	1864	1924	A popular pier demolished in 1914 with the final remains washed away in 1924
Scarborough North	300M	1869	1914	Sectioned during the war. Bomb damage, fire and storm damage lead to its demolition
Seaview Chain (IOW)	320M	1881	1952	Navy took over pier in 1945. It then went to private ownership, but a series of storms left only the pier-head intact.
Shanklin (IOW	365M	1890	1993	1987 storm destroyed sections of the pier neck and South Wight Council purchased pier for £25K and then spent £189K demolishingn it!
Sheerness	440M	1885	1960	Site of the pier is now below reclaimed land.
Southbourne	90M	1888	1909	Originally built to repeat the success of Bournemouth, gales destroyed the pier in 1900/01.
St Leonards	290M	1891	1951	Bomb damage in 1940, then a fire and severe storms in 1951.
Tenby Royal Victoria	60M	1899	1953	Demolished after falling into dis-repair during WW2.
Ventnor Royal Victoria (IOW)	205M	1873	1993	Fire damage in 1985 and 1988 lead to its demolition at a cost of £240K.
Walton on the Naze	240M	1830	1880	Walton-on-the-Naze held record for smallest resort with 2 piers. This first pier was washed away by heavy seas. The rival pier still exists.
Westward Ho	180M	1871	1880	Serious damage and unsightly appearance lead to its demolition only 9 years after its erection.
Withernsea	360M	1877	1903	Destroyed by a fishing vessel collision.

The National Piers Society

Celebrating Seaside Piers

The National Piers Society (NPS) is a UK based registered charity dedicated to promoting and sustaining interest in the preservation and continued enjoyment of seaside piers.

The Society was founded in 1979, under Sir John Betjeman, at a time when some of the UK's finest piers were threatened with demolition. Over the years the Society has grown steadily and is now established as the leading UK authority on piers. Through its efforts, several piers that would otherwise have disappeared from our coastline still remain for the enjoyment of all.

For a modest annual fee, membership is open to individuals, pier owners, local authorities and other bodies with an interest in pier preservation.

Members receive the Society's quarterly magazine 'PIERS' which provides regular news and updates on all the surviving UK piers, old photographs and postcards and details of piers overseas. Indeed, anything pertaining to piers. The Society also publishes a 'Guide to British Piers' and advises heritage bodies, lottery boards, local authorities and media on pier matters.

Eastbourne - 1997

The NPS also has an on-line shop offering a good number of pier-related books and publications as well as back issues of the NPS's own quarterly publication.

Members of the NPS are given the opportunity to vote for the Society's "Pier of the Year", (the winners are listed opposite) a prestigious award presented annually to the pier achieving the highest number of votes.

The society holds an AGM at a different pier resort each year, which also gives the opportunity for members to visit other piers in the area and an AGM dinner. This year's event was held at Southwold, with a guided tour of the pier and a visit to the two piers at Lowestoft.

In the longer term, the NPS is aiming to establish a network of regional branches and a National Pier Museum.

Further information www.piers.org.uk

My thanks to the National Piers Society and their website, which has been invaluable in my quest.

Deal - 2008

Brighton - 1998

Clevedon - 1999 & 2013

Pier of the Year

Cromer - 2000

Weston-Super-Mare Grand - 2001 & 2011

Southwold - 2002

Southport - 2003

Year	Pier
1997	Eastbourne
1998	Brighton Palace
1999	Clevedon
2000	Cromer
2001	Weston-Super-Mare Grand
2002	Southwold
2003	Southport
2004	Blackpool North
2005	Llandudno
2006	Worthing
2007	Southend-on-Sea
2008	Deal
2009	Saltburn-by-the-Sea
2010	Boscombe
2011	Weston-Super-Mare Grand
2012	Swanage
2013	Clevedon

Blackpool North - 2004

Llandudno - 2005

Worthing - 2006

Southend-on-Sea - 2007

Saltburn-by-the-Sea - 2009

Boscombe - 2010

Swanage - 2012

Further Reading

Walking over the Waves
by Chris Foote Wood

Sadly out of print now, but if you can obtain a copy it goes through the history of every surviving pier (and one that didn't), with a wonderful assortment of old images and postcards, as well as more recent photographs and a comprehensive selection of facts, figures and interesting information.

British Seaside Piers
by Chris Mawson and Richard Riding

An informative book that includes many aeriel photographs of piers (existing and lost) in their heyday, as well as an interesting array of background information.

The Great British Pier,
with photographs from the Francis Frith Collection

A fascinating pictorial journey around seaside piers at the height of their popularity, with a lively and entertaining assortment of pier facts and miscellany.

In addition, the National Piers Society web site lists a comprehensive range of books featuring piers in particular areas of the UK, individual piewwrs and a good selection of pier-related publications.

Web Sites

The National Piers Society
www.piers.org.uk

An interesting site with interesting sections on the surviving UK pleasure piers and piers that have been lost, plus a wealth of links to photographic images, postcards and pier news.

The Heritage Trail
www.theheritagetrail.co.uk

Designed to encourage people to explore Britain's heritage; the site has a large pier section with information on most of the surviving UK piers.

PS Waverley

Photographs courtesy Waverley Excursions

Paddle steamers have had a long association with the UK seaside pier. Indeed, many piers were initially constructed to provide a link between the railways and the plentiful paddle steamers available to bring additional visitors and wealth to the resorts.

These passenger steamers were a common site in Victorian times, and prospered right up to the 1970's. Their decline coincided with the UK population's new-found affinity with affordable package holidays to Europe's sunnier climes.

Named after Sir Walter Scott's first novel, the first PS Waverley was built in 1899 and served in the Second World War as a mine-sweeper, being sunk in 1940 whilst helping to evacuate troops from Dunkirk.

The current PS Waverley was built in Glasgow in 1946 as a coastal excursion paddle steamer, and is now the only existing sea-going passenger paddle steamer in the world.

The Waverley was operated by Caledonian MacBrayne (Calmac), formerly the Caledonian Steam Packet Company, until 1973 when escalating running costs meant she was retired from commercial operation. She was rescued from the scrap yard, being bought for just £1 by the Paddle Steamer Preservation Society.

Specialists and dedicated volunteers restored the Waverley to her original condition, with the help of £7m grants from various sources, including the Heritage Lottery Fund, she is now registered for up to 800 passengers.

Carrying on the great tradition of paddle steamers in years gone by, the Waverley now operates a full schedule of excursions from June to October each year from Glasgow and around the Clyde, the South Coast (including the Isle of Wight), the Bristol Channel, Kent, Essex and Suffolk.

Further information on these excursions is available at www.waverleyexcursions.co.uk

Further information on paddle steamers can be found on www.heritagesteamers.co.uk

Eastbourne

Ryde

St. Anne's

Worthing

Boscombe

94

Cleethorpes

Southwold

95